Story Building Blocks III

The Revision Layers

Diana Hurwitz

DEDICATION

To Norm for supporting my impossible dreams. To Anna and Andrew for inspiring me to dream them. To the Ladyscribes: Sharon Pielemeier, Rita Woods, Kathy Huddleston, Debbie Steinman Cameron, and Janet Skoog, for their support. To my friends for keeping me sane.

CONTENTS

Chapter 1 Introduction & Important Tools 7

Level One: Scene

Chapter 2 Scene Construction 19

Chapter 3 Cause & Effect Plot Hole 29

Chapter 4 Plausibility Plot Hole 35

Chapter 5 Redundancy Plot Hole 41

Chapter 6 Show versus Tell 45

Chapter 7 Point of View.................................... 51

Chapter 8 Tone 57

Chapter 9 Character Description 63

Chapter 10 Dialogue 69

Chapter 11 Interiority 93

Chapter 12 Body Language 99

Chapter 13 Persuasion Plot Holes 119

Chapter 14 Backstory, Dreams & Flashbacks 131

Chapter 15 Narrator Intrusion 143

Level Two: Word Choice

Chapter 16 Nouns and Pronouns 155

Chapter 17 Adjectives 167

Chapter 18 Adjectival Clauses 179

Chapter 19 Modifying Phrases 183

Chapter 20 Prepositions 189

Chapter 21 Verb Selection 191

Chapter 22 Verb Tense & Split Infinitives 197

Chapter 23 Subject Verb Agreement 207

Chapter 24 Verb Phrases 213

Chapter 25 Adverbs, Modifiers & Negation 217

Chapter 26 Conjunctions, Correlatives & Transitions ... 225

Chapter 27 Clichés, Idioms & Purple Prose 233

Chapter 28 Colloquialisms, Jargon, Slang,
& Profanity 255

Chapter 29 Redundant Words 265

Chapter 30 Similes, Metaphors & Stuff 271
Chapter 31 Interjections 283
Chapter 32 Onomatopoeia 287
Chapter 33 Sentence Structure 291
Level Three: Proofreading
Chapter 34 Capitalization 307
Chapter 35 Plurals 319
Chapter 36 Punctuation 331
Chapter 37 Use This not That 361
Chapter 38 Repetitive Words 369
Chapter 39 Formatting for Print & E Books 391
Index 409

INTRODUCTION & IMPORTANT TOOLS

Good writers craft sentences. Great writers sculpt language.

Revision adds the finishing touches to the narrative you've created. In the olden days, when traditional publishers had a talented crew of editors aboard ship, a writer had someone to suggest changes and perform the final proofreading. Nowadays, due to budget cuts, editors and proofreaders have had to walk the plank (huge mistake in my humble opinion). If your book is traditionally published, your manuscript should receive a cursory once-over and you may be asked to change things. However, traditional publishing is no longer a guarantee that your book will be solid or error-free.

Self-publishing means you must either be a good editor, know and bribe a good editor, or hire one. Hiring an editor is risky. Anyone with a fair grasp of English can hang out his shingle as an editor. If you decide to hire one, check his credentials. Ask for references. Do a criminal background check, just kidding, but only slightly. Search for him on the *Preditors & Editors* website: http://pred-ed.com.

This book will not turn you into a professional editor. For that, you need an advanced degree and a lot of experience. It will help you present a clean and tight manuscript to your agent or editor. If you self-publish, it serves as a critique partner.

I highly recommend you have several people with some knowledge of craft and grammar go over your work. I'm not suggesting other beginning writers. I'm not talking about Cousin Dick or Aunt Sally, unless they are experienced fiction writers or possess a degree in English.

Fix the plot holes, typos, and major mistakes. Then have friends, relatives, and total strangers proofread your manuscript. Pass out printed or digital copies freely and give them yellow highlighters and red pens. Don't worry; they won't steal it. They will catch things you won't. Even if your critique group critiqued your draft, the final product needs to be gone over thoroughly by people who haven't read it before. If you write in isolation, the revision layers in this book offer valuable insight.

If you self-publish, after your file is uploaded, don't hit Submit yet. Order a proof. Read it and make changes. Order a second proof. Read it and make changes. Order a third proof and check for periods, commas, and typos until you've found every error you can find. You'll be amazed at what you missed in the first and second proofs. I assure you, there will still be one or two errors in the finished product. What you want to avoid is one on every page. Errors are speed bumps that affect the reader's immersion in the story.

Revision is the most time-consuming, mind-numbing, aggravating part of writing a book. Multiple passes are required, because you can't look for everything all at once. Trust me. I've tried. There are no shortcuts. Even if you know what to avoid, you make mistakes anyway. Writing a perfect first draft takes too long. It should be full of holes. That's why they call it a *draft*. First, put your words down on paper then go back and rip them apart.

Revision passes for tone, mood, pacing, scene construction, and continuity are performed chapter by chapter. Other passes, such as searching for and killing repetitive words, are performed on the document as a whole. Working through one level at a time gets you through it and keeps you from doing something you'll regret, like burning the manuscript. You'll be tempted to quit and go spearfishing in Fiji. It only delays the inevitable.

As a special note, it is impossible to avoid repeating words. I sensed your hackles rising at the idea of cutting them. The point of checking for repetitive usage is to avoid overuse of pet phrases, weak word choices, and poor construction. It is to ensure that you repeat a word or phrase for impact rather than laziness. It means ensuring that consecutive sentences and paragraphs don't start with the same word. A proliferation of **the, and, or,** and **a** is to be expected.

Within these pages are sections on multiple parts of speech. You may not agree with the rules on what to keep and what to kill. Heaven knows the experts don't! You may be deeply attached to your darling bugaboos. Don't cut them if they mean that much to you. Keep in mind that some rules, such as sentence structure and verb tense, should not be broken. Other rules are made to be broken. Break one or two. Don't break them all. Writing rules are part of sound structure and help you avoid speed bumps and plot holes.

There are lots of lists. If there are words on those lists that you would never use, don't waste time searching for them. You may add words that aren't there. The lists are not all-inclusive. Otherwise, this book would be the size of an unabridged dictionary. No one wants to read that. The internet is an unabridged dictionary and thesaurus on steroids. Search it as often as you need to.

You will be advised to do a search and kill. Before you revise, always save a copy of your manuscript as: **"Your Title Revision 1."** Do not revise your original, ever, period. It should remain on your hard drive until all revision passes are completed. If something horrible goes wrong along the way, you might need the original paragraph or sentences. You could create a new copy for every editing pass and delete the older versions when your manuscript revision is complete. Back up daily. Back up your backup. Email it to yourself daily, if need be. Email the original to a friend for safekeeping, in case you decide to burn the manuscript and go spearfishing in Fiji.

Once you have saved the document and are ready to search and kill, hit [Control] [F] (or Find) and type the word in the box that opens. You can choose [Highlight All] and yellow highlights appear everywhere the word is found. Tackle them one by one as you scroll through the document. Alternatively, you can click on [Find Next] then click on the line in the manuscript and fix the sentence. Return to search window and click on [Find Next].This will take you to the next location. It helps to save the document often. You can save by clicking on the floppy disk icon on the drop down tool bar; [Control] [S] is faster.

Warning: A quick way of deleting a word is to use [Find] and [Replace] to replace the offensive item with another word, a space, an asterisk, or XXX. Do not do this. You end up with a document full of weird sentences. You forget what you were replacing. It creates a huge mess that gives you migraines to clean up.

The only reason to use [Find] and [Replace] is if you are changing the name of a place or character. Use [Find Next] rather than [Replace All]. Why? Here's an example. Let's say you want to replace the word *format* with *method*. The program searches for all the places the combination of letters appears. It may change words you never intended: information becomes **"in*method*ion."** If your character's name is May and you decide to change her name to Sally, you end up with, "I *sally* not want to," instead of "I may not want to." The word *maybe* becomes *sally*be. You see the problem.

If you make a mistake, [Control] [Z] or [Undo] is your best friend. It can, however, take you back further than intended. You may lose some of your recent changes. Saving after every keystroke slows you down too much, so I don't advise it. You should save the file frequently enough, perhaps at the end of each page, to mitigate heartache if your computer goes haywire, turns off in the middle, or you unintentionally select [Undo]. Weird things happen.

Your new critique partner, if you haven't met her yet, is the [Word Options] section. Click on the [Word] icon at the top left of the screen in *Word 1997-2003* (or File in newer versions of *Word for Windows*). A menu drops down in which you can select [New]. [Save], etc. Most of us are familiar with those options. What many haven't explored is the [Word Options] section. It was unexplored territory to me before I formatted files for E-books and had to turn off [Automatic Formatting]. If you have been frustrated with *Word* for doing things you didn't want it to do, or for changing things you preferred not be changed, this is your culprit.

[Word Options] unleashes a wealth of useful tools. Do not write your draft with these tools on. It slows you down to a crawl. For the purposes of revision, it helps to turn on all the options. When you save a copy to format for E-books, [Automatic Formatting] must be turned off.

[Automatic Formatting] is the thing that changes **cliche** to **cliché.** It is the mastermind behind spell checking and leaves all those squiggly red and green lines most of us ignore. It also creates line returns, font styles, spacing, paragraph formatting, and numbering. It encodes the formatting you must eliminate from the E-book copy.

To explore the options, click on the [Word] icon (or File) at the upper left corner of the screen. Go to the bottom of the drop-down menu and click on [Word Options] (or Options). Scroll down the drop-down menu and click on [Proofing]. In *Word 1993-2007,* scroll down the drop-down menu to [Writing Styles] and change [Grammar Only] to [Grammar & Styles]. Click on [Settings] and you have access to the full toolkit. In later versions of *Word,* the menu box is set up a little bit differently. There are options below the [Automatic Correction] options to explore first and other tabs that open when you select the [Automatic Correction] option. The theory remains the same.

In *Word 1993-2007*, the first section is [Require].

◈Comma required before last item (select always or don't check).

◈Punctuation required with quotes (select inside, outside, or don't check).

◈Spaces required between sentences (select 1, 2, or don't check). Using typewriters required two. The answer in modern times is one.

Selecting these options does not remove the need to proofread after you've turned them on.

The second section is [Grammar]. You can select or unselect the following (select them all):

- ☑ capitalization
- ☑ fragments and run-ons
- ☑ misused words
- ☑ negation
- ☑ noun phrases
- ☑ possessives and plurals

- ☑ punctuation
- ☑ questions
- ☑ relative clauses
- ☑ subject-verb agreement
- ☑ verb phrases.

The third section is [Style]. You can select or unselect the following:

- ☑ clichés, colloquialisms, and jargon
- ☑ contractions
- ☑ fragments
- ☑ gender specific words
- ☑ numbers
- ☑ passive sentences
- ☑ possessives and plurals
- ☑ punctuation
- ☑ relative clauses
- ☑ sentence length
- ☑ sentence structure

- ☑ sentences beginning with but
- ☑ successive nouns (more than 3)
- ☑ successive prepositional phrases
- ☑ unclear phrasing
- ☑ use of first person
- ☑ verb phrases (stylistic suggestions)
- ☑ wordiness
- ☑ words in split infinitives (more than one)

Select them all. You have the option to ignore the program's advice as you investigate each instance.

These tools help you identify problems as you complete the revision passes we discuss in this book. As you read through, right click on the items underlined in green. Suggestions appear. You can change the words or ignore the rule. I suggest ignoring it **once** rather than **always**. You can ignore it throughout the entire manuscript if it is something that you are doing deliberately, like misspelling a name, etc. Remember to turn them off when you have finished revising.

The revision of a book can take a writer from one who writes for pleasure to one who writes with intention and mastery. This compilation of collected wisdom is derived from the file folder full of notes from articles, conferences, and **How To** books that spanned many years. When it was time to revise a new novel, I decided to combine all of the Post-Its, aging notepaper pages, and computer files into one location so I could easily find them again. In the process, I expanded the lists and added current theories. I hope this information helps you as much as it helps me. Writers should help other writers craft polished fiction.

Diana Hurwitz

LEVEL ONE: SCENE

Scenes don't just happen in movies. They happen when you turn on and manipulate your verbal camera. Your narrator's eyes take in and process everything said and done in his vicinity.

Writing screenplays and writing fiction are two entirely different processes. This book addresses fiction, not screenwriting. However, you want the reader to experience your written story as smoothly and intently as a video story. You must consider the timeline, be careful how you transition, and make sure every scene you write earns its page time. You must choose when to cut action and move to the next scene. Your choice of where and when and how to reveal information is crucial. You choose which details are important enough to impart. You must consider line of sight, perspective, mood, atmosphere, and physical choreography.

When you assign characters a role and dialogue, they become method actors. They utilize motivation and body language. Your "actors" must be realistic. The biggest difference is that you can access your character's interior world through your words in a way the screen cannot. Your character can think and talk to himself, which adds subtlety to the conflicts. Narrative passages illustrate your story world. Descriptions paint scenery and backdrops.

You must set the scene and *show* your reader the things a video camera would record. You picture everything in your mind and choose the right words to convey what you see. Rhetorical devices and word choices add the 3-D effect to your story world.

You are the writer, director, actor, scene designer, prop handler, and producer. It's a lot of work. It's worth it, or you wouldn't be reading this book.

SCENE CONSTRUCTION

What constitutes a scene? A scene is specific characters in one location going after a specific goal at a specific time.

■ Characters can enter and exit a scene. If you switch from one point of view to another, it is best to change scenes.

■ Characters can change locations, such as from room to room, while going about the scene objective. The reader does not need to hear about every pit stop, meal, and clothes change between scenes. If a character flies from New York to Chicago, the scene ends in New York as he boards the airplane. A new scene begins in Chicago. The exception is a scene in which the airplane ride is part of the plot. An airplane could act as the setting for a scene.

If you focus on mundane things such as meals, personal hygiene, commutes, and routine work, you should have a compelling reason for telling us about it. An overall story problem could force an obsessively neat character to stop caring about cleanliness. If so, show him scrubbing the bathroom sink at the beginning and walking away from a dirty one at the end. Don't use daily drudgeries to drag out the page count.

A scene changes when the timeline changes. If the cops are planning a stakeout in the morning and perform the stakeout in the evening, the scene ends in the morning. A new scene begins in the evening.

A scene should open with a hook followed by transitions orienting the reader to the change in time, place, point of view, and a description of setting. Where are we? When is it? Who is present? What is going on? You should provide enough detail to orient the reader in the scene, but not so much that his eyes glaze over. You can begin with narrative, dialogue, or action. The choice is yours. Each method has strengths and weaknesses. Variation is better than monotony.

Your point of view character should have a goal in mind when the scene starts. When you sit down to write a scene, your characters do and say things. What they do and say should have purpose. Their actions and words should move the story forward or cause complications and reversals.

A scene can contain action, dialogue, internal dialogue, gestures, thoughts, reactions, back-story, description, or narrative. The most important points to consider are what the character wants, what motivates him, and whether he succeeds or fails. Every character you follow with your verbal camera should be up to something. It may not be entirely clear what his purpose is, but he should be pursuing an objective.

A scene should have overt or subtle tension. Every scene should make another scene necessary. This keeps the reader turning pages.

Each scene can end with an intriguing final sentence, or hook, that makes the reader want to begin the next chapter. The opening and closing hooks can be inserted during the revision phase.

Let's consider items to look for in your scenes during the revision pass.

Actions and reactions: Your characters' actions and reactions should follow a logical order. If Dick plans to stab Jane, he has to find her. The weapon must be available. Dick picks it up, aims it, strikes, reacts, and recovers. Test the choreography of your scene. Does it work? Does it flow? How long does it take? Is it physically possible? Have the physical involuntary reactions come before the verbal and conscious physical reactions? Act the scene out. Better yet, have other people act it out. Are you feeling it? Are you laughing, crying, worrying, or shivering? Watch out for disruptive action reversals where an action occurs, subsequent actions occur, then you revisit the initial action.

Clichés: Are your characters' actions and dialogue new and fresh, or a bit on the stale side? There are few new things under the sun. How you relate them can make them feel new. Are your plot devices new or overused? Are they clichés?

Complexity: As an exercise, save a copy of your manuscript and cut everything but the main story line. Does it hold its own? Do the same for each subplot. Do they stand alone? Do they work together to form a satisfying whole, or are there so many strands the plot is hard to follow? Cut nonessential scenes. If you have a short, linear story with no additional threads, your structure may not be complex enough.

Dead zones: If you cannot pinpoint the conflict and resolution in your scene, you have a plot hole. If people are talking and moving, but nothing is accomplished, you have created a dead zone. Conflict can be extremely subtle, but it needs to be there. Dead zones make readers put your book down or flip pages.

The viewpoint character you follow with your verbal camera in the scene should have an objective and either succeed or fail. Other characters in the scene may have their own objectives. The conflict can be internal, external, antagonistic, or interpersonal. Dick might need to interview a suspect, talk to his wife about money, or desperately need a smoke and a cup of coffee. People and events conspire to keep him from getting the cigarette break or prevent him from having the necessary conversation.

Devices that hook: To keep the reader invested, use boundary violations, cliffhangers, complications, denial of core needs, difficult decisions, dilemmas, emotional compromises, epiphanies, physical danger, resource limitations, revelations, or space limitations. Every scene should contain something that encourages the readers to care about what happens next. Use these devices for effect. Employ one per scene, not one per paragraph.

Goalposts: Think of a scene as having an object and a verb. The object of the story problem or scene goal is the target or focus of the words and actions: person, place, thing, information, situation, physical task, mental task, need, want, emotion, belief, or prejudice. The verb of the story problem or scene goal is the motion toward or away from the object.

In reference to the object, the character should want to: obtain or get rid of, hold onto or release, reach or escape, reveal or hide, change or keep from changing, tell or not tell, evade or capture, avert or allow, define or obscure, prove or disprove, evaluate or decide.

The goal of the antagonist, or antagonistic forces, is to keep the protagonist from obtaining the object and make the verb difficult, if not impossible. The friends and foes provide stumbling blocks and step ladders to keep the character moving toward and away from the scene object and make the verb more difficult or easier. If you cannot identify your scene object and verb, you have a plot hole.

In media res: This means starting your scene when the situation gets interesting, not before. It means cutting out the inconsequential details and focusing on the actions and interactions that matter.

■ **Narrative summary**: How long is it? Is it serving a specific purpose? It should add to, extend, delay, reveal, or obscure the content of the scene. It can set up a scene. It can prolong a scene. It can end a scene. It should reveal character or add mood and atmosphere. You may need to use narrative to transition into a scene to address a time lapse or change in point of view. Use it to open a scene when you need to wrinkle time. Make sure it leads into action and dialogue instead of taking up pages at a time. Narrative is slow, use a paragraph or two to offer resting beats.

■ **Outcome**: For every goal, there is an outcome. The character can succeed in his goal and feel good about it or bad about. He can achieve his goal only to find out it was the wrong goal. He can achieve his goal and find he has created a bigger problem. The character can fail and feel good about it or bad about it. The character can fail and realize he was after the wrong goal, so his failure was really a success. He can get distracted, blocked, or delayed and have to try again in a future scene.

■ **Save the best for last:** People remember best what they heard last. By giving the most important information last, you create suspense. The image you leave them with is the one they remember, whether it is at the end of the scene or the book. The same is true of sentences in a paragraph as well as paragraphs on a page.

■ **Setting errors**: Does the reader know when it is and where it is? Have you oriented him to the scene? Have you described the setting enough that he can envision the room, the park, or the weather conditions? You may decide to open a scene with setting to transport the reader to a new place and time. It should be powerful and necessary. The description should evoke the emotion and atmosphere of the circumstances. The scene can start out with one emotion and end on another.

Speed: You need to provide the reader with satisfying S-curves. You do so by adjusting your foot on the plot gas peddle with word choice and sentence structure.

Slow speed consists of a blend of description, narrative, and exposition. It uses physical and psychological description to set the mood. Internal dialogue is slow. Long cumulative sentences are slow. Blocks of narrative and internal thoughts are slow. Facts, review, summary, back-story, and flashbacks are slow. Journals and letters are extremely slow. The focus is broad.

Medium speed consists of transitions, step by step detail, dialogue, and action that lead up to the core confrontation. Anxiety is created. Will they or won't they? Can they or can't they? It uses compound sentences with limited detail. It uses fleshed out dialogue interposed with action beats and short internal thoughts. Focus shifts toward a specific encounter or activity.

High speed consists of dialogue with lots of white space. Short summary can be fast. The verbal camera pans quickly over it.

Top speed consists of short dialogue or action beats without narrative description. Blow by blow action with short sentences is very fast. Rapid-fire dialogue is very fast. Focus narrows to a pinpoint.

Look at the composition of your paragraphs and scenes. Did you vary the speed within the scene? It can start slow and build momentum. It can start fast and slow down. It can start fast, slow down, and build back up. Draw a line representing the flow of your scene. What does it look like?

If your scene is nonstop action without resting beats, it is too fast. If your scene lacks action beats or is all internal thoughts and narrative, it is too slow. Highlight the fast parts. Are there peaks and valleys? Make sure you have quieter and slower conflicts between the big turning points and reveals.

Suspense: Suspense is what happens before the bang. It is the tension leading up to the reveal. This is true whether you are writing a Thriller action sequence or a Literary conversation. The characters fight, striking and parrying until the knock out punch. The characters banter, lobbing and parrying until the killing comment strikes. The characters run, dodging and tripping as they flee the monster.

Every tense action scene should have a rise, impact, and fall. Every conversation should contain tension. If the conversation is the scene obstacle, it should build up to a tense exchange, a verbal zinger, and a response. To stretch the tension, zoom in beat by beat. To compress the tension, summarize. Show the recovery. Leave with a hook illustrating the new complication.

Timing Errors: Your description of the action should not take longer to read than it did to occur.

Jane dodged the blade, her arms wheeling, her muscles quivering as Dick swung his sword.

Chances are, the sword is faster than Jane's ability to outrun it. You also have Jane dodging before Dick swings. To fix it, reword it.

Dick swung the sword. Jane fell back. The blade missed her chest.

Describe actions in the order they occur so the reader isn't seeing things happen twice. Don't jerk the reader forward and backward. Having to reread a passage creates a speed bump. Action should move forward. Don't backfill. Be wary of the words *after* and *before*.

Revision Tips

✍ When your manuscript is finished, go back and highlight the opening and closing lines. Does the opening line set up the conflict for the scene? Does the ending line offer a hook that keeps the reader turning the page?

✍ Does your scene goal contain an object and verb?

✍ Does the choreography flow smoothly?

✍ Are the actions and reactions in the right order?

✍ Did you vary the speed?

✍ Did you invoke the mood and atmosphere you intended?

✍ Highlight the descriptions. Did you fill in the setting?

✍ Does your scene contain tension?

✍ Does your scene contribute to the overall story or subplot?

CAUSE & EFFECT PLOT HOLE

Every scene should lead to the next scene. Causality is an event (the cause) that creates another event (the effect). Taking away one of the steps renders the rest unnecessary or impossible.

If convicted of robbing a bank (cause), you go to jail (effect), which causes you to find a way to escape (cause), which puts you on the run (effect), which causes you to search for proof that you are innocent.

A cause can be an object, information, situation, conversation, or an encounter. There are intentional and unintentional causes that have intentional and unintentional effects. The effect can be immediate. The effect can be delayed and only in hindsight does the connection become clear.

If Dick receives an object in Chapter 2, he is forced to do something with it in Chapter 3.

✎If Dick receives information that overturns what he believed in Chapters 1 through 10, it changes how he thinks in Chapters 11 through 20.

✎ If Dick has a conversation with Sally in Chapter 2, the ramifications of that conversation may not be apparent until Chapter 12.

✎ If Dick encounters an old friend in Chapter 5, it may change his outlook on the story problem in the remaining chapters.

A cause could have a number of effects or ripples that aren't obvious at first. We do not exist in a vacuum.

✎ Dick's seemingly innocent decision in Chapter 1 can have unforeseen consequences in the final stretch of the story. Dick might have decided that flirting with the secretary at the company picnic was harmless in Chapter 4, someone mentions it to his wife in Chapter 6, and she files for divorce in Chapter 18.

A cause could create different effects for different people.

✎ Dick's seemingly innocent decision in Chapter 1 might cause serious ripples for Sally and Jane. Dick may have made the right choice, but it has negative consequences for those around him. Friends and family often become targets or victims in Horror and Thriller tales. Dick's decision to confront the horror is the cause. The death of his friends is the unintentional effect.

Each scene should make the next scene necessary.

✎ If Dick decides to steal a painting in Chapter 1, he encounters obstacles to obtaining it. He cases the museum in Chapter 3 and finds out there are more guards than he counted back in Chapter 2. He learns the details of the security system in Chapter 6. He realizes the caper will be harder than he imagined. He then must push himself beyond his comfort zone. He talks to an expert in Chapter 7. His plot is overheard. His first attempt in Chapter 10 fails. Dick is forced to back off and try again. His initial attempt alerted the museum guard, so Dick must be sneakier or bolder on his second attempt.

In Chapter 15, Dick arrives at the museum to find the person that overheard his plot is there before him. The alarm sounds. Dick escapes, but is now forced to try a third time. The museum guards are on high alert, which makes the caper impossible to pull off. Dick decides to go through with it anyway. His fourth attempt in Chapter 20 goes sideways because they beefed up security. He is nearly caught. At the last minute in Chapter 21, he gets away with or without the painting. Each failed attempt made the next obstacle more difficult to overcome.

At scene level, no one does anything just because. They have a motive for everything they do, from getting up in the morning to why they fight vampires. It's a plot hole when you have a character do something because the plot called for it, especially when it is out of character. This relates to the plausibility plot hole. Instead of whether or not it *could*

31

really happen, it is a problem of whether or not it *should* have happened in the way that it did.

Readers sense when the plot does not add up logically. You can't have a story wherein people can't fly and decide at the climax that your protagonist can fly. You haven't set up a world in which people fly, so the device is out of place.

☙ If Dick is dysfunctional enough to hate small children, he is not miraculously going to love them by the end of the book. He may have learned to tolerate them, but he won't embrace them. People rarely change that much. Base personality traits rarely change to any significant degree unless there is brain damage.

☙ If Dick sips cocktails at a party and suddenly goes crazy, knocks drinks off trays, curses, and throws a fit, you must set up the reason for it. He had to see something that triggered a memory or horrific realization, or someone slipped him hallucinogenic drugs and he is seeing angry bees.

For every action, there is a reaction.

☙ If Dick does something stupid, funny, or unusual, someone in the room notices. His behavior has ripples. The immediate effect is that people cut off conversations to stare. Security may escort him outside. Men arriving in a white truck may haul him off. People gossip about his unusual behavior to other people. It may be important that someone noticed he was there.

Nowhere is cause and effect more evident than in the spread of information. Someone tells someone who tells someone. Most criminals and liars are caught this way.

To see if your scenes pass the cause and effect test, examine the conflict at the heart of each scene. Does the complication in each scene make something else in the story inevitable? It should. The worse kind of filler is having scenes in which characters talk and act but do nothing to further the plot or set up complications. The cause might not be obvious right away. It dawns on the reader when the effect is revealed.

Revision Tips

✍ If you haven't already done so, list the central conflict in each scene or chapter.

✍ What cause have you planted in that scene?

✍ In which scene is the effect felt?

✍ If the scene contains neither cause nor effect, do you need it? If you can't cut it, repair the plot hole.

✍ If your character does something in the scene, what is the immediate effect? What cause led up to his actions? If you can't pinpoint the cause and the effect, you have some revision to do.

PLAUSIBILITY PLOT HOLE

Plausibility means ensuring the actions and reactions of your characters are believable. Every reader agrees to suspend disbelief when she sits down with your story. Fiction is not what really happens. Fiction is what happens in the story world you created. You create the rules and reality. Most genres work within the realm of what is truly possible in this world at the time in which is it set. A writer has the freedom to tweak it slightly, as long as he does not strain credibility.

Plausibility plot holes occur when you haven't done your homework or set up your story world properly. Research is crucial whether you are writing a contemporary Romance or a prairie Western. To fix these plot holes, research and fact check. Nitpickers are out there waiting for you. If you can't visit the place, get maps of the location and guidebooks. Talk to someone who lives there. Read articles and blogs about the time and place. Look at books, photographs, paintings, drawings, or diagrams. Read newspaper archives to get a feel for the way a particular populace wrote and spoke. What were their customs, morals, and slang? If you write Science Fiction and Fantasy, craft these details to suit your story.

You decide how earth-like your fantasy world is. You design the terrain, the weather patterns, government and social systems, currency, rituals, theology, clothing, and transportation. Most writers try to keep it similar to earth so they don't have to reinvent the wheel. You should explain your world well and abide by the rules you have created. If you are not writing Fantasy or Science Fiction, all of these details still matter.

Historical inaccuracies are plot holes. Ancient Greece did not have stock car races. The average man and woman have never been on the moon. Mankind did not saddle up dinosaurs. Settings should be accurate and correspond to the historical period, whether it is 1482 or 2002.

Line of sight is a common plausibility error. Think about where your verbal camera is perched at all times. Are you looking through the POV character's eyes? Is your verbal camera perched on his shoulder? Are you using an omniscient camera that can zoom anywhere at any time? You can't see through walls, unless you are paranormal. You can't see behind yourself, unless you are looking in a mirror. You can't see into another room, inside another building, or into the next town. You can't read minds, unless you are telepathic. You can make judgment calls based on a person's expression and posture, but your judgment could be wrong.

You can tweak reality slightly. There may not be a Cygnet Committee running New York City, but there could be. There may not be a terrorist cell operating in San Francisco, but there could be. Those are plausible scenarios. A reader may find it hard to believe the entire world is unaware of a seething underbelly of paranormal creatures. It may have been plausible in 1600 A.D. It is highly unlikely that monstrous creatures would go unnoticed in 2012 with satellites and cameras everywhere. Superman might be able to leap tall buildings in a single bound, but a Boston cop can't. Even in Fantasy and Science Fiction, the rules of physics still apply.

Plausibility plot holes occur when your character's voice is inconsistent or doesn't ring true. If you write about a thirty-year-old woman, she should not sound like a twelve-year-old boy. Commercials where a female teen identity thief's voice comes out of a fifty-year-old man are hilarious. It doesn't work in fiction.

It is a cringe-inducing plausibility hole when toddlers think like adults and speak in full, lyrical sentences. If you do not have the right-aged child around to listen to, go to the mall and hang out near the play area. Listen to the children talk. From age two onward, their vocabularies increase and their thought processes mature. They are brutally honest and repeat everything they hear. Two does not sound like five. Five does not sound like twelve.

Men and women communicate differently. They choose different words. Someone in New York will not sound like someone in Louisiana. Someone born in 1800 will not talk like someone born in 2012.

Which leads to: plausibility plot holes occur when the story is not grounded in psychology. An introvert does not become an extrovert overnight. The way women perceive things and the way men perceive things are very different. The way a rigid person views things and the way a fuzzy person views things are entirely different. A character born 1700 would view our world quite differently than a character born in 2000.

Psychological integrity is the subject matter of *Story Building Blocks II: Crafting Believable Conflict* as well as my blog *Game On!* Your characters act and react for a reason. Make sure you understand it, even if they don't.

Revision Tips

Are you characters behaving "out of character?" If so, you need a really good reason and it has to be set up before they do so.

Have you created rules for your Fantasy or Science Fiction world? Have you been consistent?

Orient yourself in the scene. Think about what you can see, smell, hear, taste, and touch. Is there anything that doesn't belong in your scene?

✍ Are your characters acting and reacting in ways that are plausible for the history you have given them? Have they defied physics or rationality?

✍ Do the characters speak the way they should?

Diana Hurwitz

REDUNDANCY PLOT HOLES

In Composition 101, we were taught that every sentence should further the proposition of a paragraph and every paragraph should further the proposition of the thematic statement. We crafted outlines with topics and subtopics. The paper opened with a thematic statement. It explored topic one followed by topic two. Each subtopic furthered the proposition of the topic by expanding it, supporting it, or refuting it. It concluded by restating your position on the thematic argument.

Dogs make great pets. Dogs come in many breeds. Some breeds make better pets than others. Herding breeds are protective of their owners. Herding dogs make great pets.

When writing fiction, the progression of ideas is equally important. Redundant information reveals are plot holes that rewind the story unnecessarily. They work like this:

The story opens by explaining: There is a water shortage. People are dying.

In Chapter Two, more people discuss it: There is a very serious water shortage. People are dying.

In Chapter Three, the topic is rehashed without adding anything to it.

There is no progression of ideas. There is no twist or reversal to the original statement. It is beating your reader over the head with a big stick. To fix redundancy plot holes, offer new information in each chapter.

Chapter One: There is a water shortage, people are frightened.

Chapter Two: One of the reservoirs has been poisoned. More people will die.

Chapter Three: They come up with a plan to seed the clouds to make it rain.

◂◂ Revealing the same information through two separate characters is redundant. In Chapter One, Dick and Jane face an obstacle and overcome it. We hear about it from his point of view. In Chapter Two, we hear about the same event from Jane's point of view. The author has taken us back in time to rehash old information. Even if Jane saw things differently, we already know how they overcame the obstacle. Jane can summarize her alternate view of what happened, but she needs to move on to a different obstacle in her scene and keep the time line moving forward. Stories that bend, twist, and stagger a timeline still have to offer a new proposition in each scene. Each "revelation" needs to reveal something different.

◄◄ Revealing the same information through dialogue more than once is redundant. Dick may tell Jane something and eventually have to explain it to Sally. However, the second reveal should twist, refute, add to, or extend the original proposition. The reader should know Dick is holding something back or telling something new. It is okay for a detective and his team to take a moment to review the evidence together to gain fresh insight. It is not okay for a couple of friends to rehash the same topic five times without movement.

◄◄ Plot devices can be redundant. If your character is being tortured, sword fighting, or having sex in every scene, it becomes monotonous. It is especially annoying when a plot device is inserted because the script called for it.

Revision Tips

✍ Look at the conflict at the heart of each scene separately. Is it new or a repeat of something that has already been done or said?

✍ If you don't cut it, can you twist it? It should serve a valid purpose other than to take up space.

✍ Look at the proposition in each paragraph. Is it new? Do the subsequent paragraphs support, refute, extend, or twist it?

SHOW VERSUS TELL

Show versus tell sounds complicated, because it is. It is hotly debated whether you should ever summarize by telling rather than showing. If you tell something, the reader processes the information through your filter. If you show something, he processes the information through the character's filter.

Narrative summary shouldn't *tell*. Sometimes you have to provide important background, condense time, and relate events that don't deserve a lot of page time. Theoretically, it should be done through the character's filter, not the writer's. Summary shouldn't regurgitate what has been said. It should support, extend, or refute a proposition. It can add context in a timely fashion and set up expectation. It uses a few words that work hard and lead into or trail action and dialogue. If narrative runs on for paragraphs or pages, you have some editing to do.

Narrative transitions between scenes:

Dick skipped the shower and shave and was at the crime scene by nine thirty. He stood next to the corpse lying on the ground. He obviously hadn't shaved either and the bath in the river hadn't done him any favors.

Narrative wrinkles time:

The next week was brutal. Dick tackled the stacks of paperwork he had successfully ignored for a month. He drank gallons of coffee and smoked endless packs of cigarettes. His anxiety grew like a bonfire as he waited for the DNA results.

Narrative should not become an information dump. Info dumps are often found in prologues, epilogues, summaries of what happened in previous books, long dialogue passages, *as you know* dialogue, long explanations of how things work, extensive backstory, and all of Grimm's fairytales. Entire novels were written in narrative summary before the turn of the century.

Narrative skips over the boring bits. Shift it into real-time when possible, particularly if you find paragraphs of it. Use specific details and strong word choices.

Showing is illustrated through actions and interiority rather than adjectives and adverbs.

Action: Don't tell us what a character does. Don't write: *Dick worked hard.* Show us what constitutes working hard. Show him working up a sweat, straining his muscles, etc.

Emotions: Don't tell us what the character feels. Don't write: *Jane felt sad.* Show her sitting down at a desk. She stares at the coffee ring on the scarred surface. She traces it with her finger. She wipes a tear from her cheek.

Description: Don't tell us a character is (insert generic adjective - ugly, pretty, fat, thin). Describe her in a fresh, not cliché, way. What about her is pretty or ugly? What does the point of view character consider pretty or ugly? What is attractive to one person might not be to another.

Telling often involves adverbs and adjectives. Look for bland descriptive words like: ***attractive, dumb, embarrassing, fabulous, fascinating, handsome, hilarious, mad, powerful, pretty, smart, stunning, stupid, tired,*** and ***ugly***. Make it fresh. Telling is fertile ground for clichés.

Examples of bad telling:

Telling: Dick was a powerfully built man. He drew everyone's attention when he entered the room.

Showing: Dick strode into the bar. The crowd parted to allow him through. Conversations stopped mid-sentence. His wide shoulders brushed onlookers as he passed, sloshing the beer from their mugs.

Telling: Dick was tired.

Showing: Dick slumped in the recliner, kicked off his loafers, and loosened his tie. He stared at the blank television screen. He didn't bother to turn it on.

Telling: The problem was obvious; Dick had no idea how to handle the situation.

Showing: Dick scratched his neck. What now?

Author intrusion is bad telling and is covered in Chapter 15.

Revision Tips

✍ Read through your manuscript. Highlight areas that contain narrative. Decide whether you should turn narrative into action and dialogue. If not, is it serving a distinct purpose? Does it support, extend, add to, or refute a proposition? Does it condense time or provide important background?

✍ Does it involve tertiary characters or actions that are of lesser importance?

✍ Does it involve clichés?

✍ Have you told the reader what someone thinks or feels instead of showing it?

POINT OF VIEW

Plot holes occur when it is unclear whose thoughts are represented. If the reader can't easily identify who is talking or thinking, he must stop and re-read the passage. Do it once or twice, and he'll forgive you; do it often and he stops reading your book.

It is best to pick a style of viewpoint and stick with it throughout the story. You alternate point of view characters by changing the position of your verbal camera. You should stick with one character's point of view per scene. Switching viewpoint from sentence to sentence or paragraph to paragraph creates confusion. It is called **head-hopping**. Readers forgive an occasional transgression, but stop reading if it happens often. Once or twice in a story is forgiven. Once or twice in a paragraph isn't.

Using one viewpoint keeps the reader inside the main character's head throughout. Alternating two viewpoints presents an opportunity for suspense, particularly in Thriller and Suspense and Mystery. The author can follow the protagonist, antagonist, and several secondary characters. It is important to note that you dilute the reader's emotional connection to the story with every viewpoint you add. If you use multiple viewpoints, make them count and limit it to the main characters.

In addition to the number of viewpoint characters, you have to choose which type of viewpoint you wish to use: first person, second person, or third person. Each method has strengths and weaknesses.

If you choose first person, you always follow the viewpoint character with your verbal camera. If you use third person, the verbal camera can follow a different character in each chapter or scene.

It is important to note that not every story is told through the protagonist's point of view. Sometimes it is a friend, a foe, or a narrator. In most genre fiction, a protagonist viewpoint is preferred. Stories are rarely told by the antagonist. It is difficult to root for a protagonist only seen through the antagonist's eyes.

There are many articles and books on writing the different points of view. I will touch on the main categories briefly.

📽 In the First Person method, the reader experiences the story through the protagonist's lens. The verbal camera records through the character's eyes. The reader experiences, and is limited to, what the protagonist sees, hears, smells, tastes, feels, and could know about. The story is influenced by his outlook on things. He must be in every scene. You can't have the antagonist talking to his cohort unless the protagonist is present to see and/or overhear them. This can be limiting, but adds a depth to the story other methods lack. The reader becomes the protagonist. He experiences the character's thoughts and feelings firsthand. I like this method. It has a sense of immediacy other methods lack. As a reader I like becoming the character. Some readers hate it.

This method uses *I, me, mine.*

One of the difficulties of first person is avoiding an overabundance of sentences with *I, me,* and *my.* It requires stringent editing and inventive descriptions of the point of view character.

Some stories are written with shifting first person point of view. The important point with this method is to stick with one viewpoint per scene. It is essential to orient the reader to the change of viewpoint at the beginning of the scene so the reader knows whose head he is in.

📽 In First Person Subjective, the point of view character is the narrator, but he relates his version of someone else's story. The story is told through his filter and can limit the suspense potential. The verbal camera records through this observer's eyes. It is limited to what he can see, hear, etc. You cannot explore anyone else's thoughts unless they voice them.

This is told in first person using *I, me,* and *mine.*

This is limited to one point of view character who expounds on what he believes is going on. He is often a friend or foe, such as Dr. Watson in *Sherlock Holmes.* The way this character views the events reveals who he really is, what he thinks, feels, and believes. He isn't necessarily a reliable narrator.

📽 In the Modified Objective Third Person, a point of view character might not know what the other characters are thinking, but puts his own spin on it.

This is told in third person using *he, she,* and *they.*

The point of view character interprets what is happening through the filter of his beliefs and feelings. If the viewpoint belongs to someone other than the protagonist, the narrator can mislead the reader. When the reader realizes he has been led astray, he feels cheated. It is hard to summon the requisite empathy for the protagonist when the story is told from someone else's viewpoint. It's like listening to someone read you a story rather than experiencing it for yourself.

🎥 In the Objective Third Person, also referred to as Third Person Close Up, you tell the story from the viewpoint of a verbal camera that sits on a character's shoulder. It records whatever the viewpoint character sees and hears. The camera can move from one character to another.

It is similar to first person but uses *she, he,* and *they.*

This method allows you to pan away from the protagonist and follow different characters to record their interactions. The advantage is, you can give the reader information the protagonist is unaware of.

It is best to limit the point of view to one character per scene or chapter to avoid confusing your reader. This works well in stories where the reader finds out what the antagonist is up to before the protagonist does. It heightens the suspense.

🎥 The Omniscient point of view is done with an objective narrator that knows all, sees all, and reads every mind at any given time. This verbal camera pans the scenes from afar. There are few limitations as to where it can zoom and what it can record. The downside is, it feels distant to the reader. This was popular in early British literature, but is very difficult to execute successfully.

This is done with *he, she,* and *they.*

The challenge is shifting the vantage point of the verbal camera so that you don't make the reader dizzy. It is important that it not be random and that the reader is alerted to the shift from one person to another. It notoriously results in head-hopping. The other danger with this method is consistency. It is difficult to stay in this point of view and not veer off into first person or third person close up.

Revision Tips

✍ How many viewpoint characters are you following? Have you used them only once or twice? Are they essential to the plot or can you rework their scenes from a main character's point of view?

✍ Did you stick with one viewpoint in the scene?

✍ Is it clear which point of view character is thinking or acting? Did you transition appropriately? Have you head-hopped?

✍ Read your draft. Are the point of view characters consistent throughout? Are his attitude, language, history, etc. consistent?

Diana Hurwitz

TONE

A child learns early on to recognize tone of voice. The mother's soft, sweet coo means she is happy with him. The low growl utilizing his middle name means he pushed the boundaries a tad too far, but what does tone have to do with fiction?

Tone is the emotional atmosphere the writer establishes and maintains throughout the entire novel based on how the point of view character feels about the information he relates. You may not have thought about how you actually feel about your story. Take a moment to consider. Are you writing about ghosts with a wink and a nudge or are you aiming for chill bumps? Is the story serious and bittersweet or a satirical exposé?

Tone can be formal or informal, light or dark, grave or comic, impersonal or personal, subdued or passionate, reasonable or irrational, plain or ornate. The narrator can be cynical, sarcastic, sweet, or funny. A satirical and caustic tone plays well in a Comedy. It won't play well in a cozy Mystery.

❦ Tone should suit genre. Are you writing a shallow Chick Lit comedy or a dark and mysterious Gothic novel? If you write a mixed genre, the tone should match the genre that takes precedence over the other.

If you are writing a funny romance, you have to decide if you want your reader to belly laugh her way through it or have a few moments that make her belly laugh while worrying about the outcome of the relationship. Some Romance fans love the frothy, light tone of Chick Lit. Others prefer the melodramatic tone of Historical Romance. Yet another prefers a heart-wrenching Literary love story.

Some paranormal stories are eerie and set an ominous tone. Light Horror feels almost comic to the reader. Readers who prefer ominous, creepy paranormal might not enjoy the comical version.

❦ Tone is demonstrated by word choice and the way you reveal the details. It illustrates the narrator's attitude toward the characters and the situation. If he does not take the characters or situation seriously, the reader won't either. Word choice, syntax, imagery, sensory cues, level of detail, depth of information, and metaphors reveal tone.

❦ Tone is not the same as voice. Stephen King writes horror. His voice is distinct. At times he employs quirky, adolescent boy humor, but his aim is to chill you. A writer a bit heavy-handed with the humor can ruin a good horror story.

❧ Tone is not the same as mood. Tone is how the character feels about the scene. Mood is the atmosphere you set for the reader. If you are writing a mystery, a scene can be brooding and dark leading up to the sleuth finding the body. The mood can lighten as the detectives indulge in a moment of gallows humor. The tone defines your mystery as wisecracking noir or cozy British.

❧ Tone is not the same as style. Style is revealed through sentence structure, use of literary devices, rhythm, jargon, slang, and accents. Style is revealed through dialogue. Style showcases the background and education of the characters. It expresses the character's belief system, opinions, likes, and dislikes. It is controlled by what the characters say and how they say it. Tone is revealed by the narrator's perceptions, what he chooses to explore, and what he chooses to hide.

♥ You are writing a Romance. Let's say Dick, your narrator, is at a company picnic in a park. The sky is clear. The grill is smoking. His coworkers are drinking beer and it is mid afternoon. How does Dick feel about being there? If he is an extrovert and happy with his job, he is lightheartedly milling around, joking, laughing, and downing brews with the best of them. He has a great time, until he learns something that turns his happy place into a not so happy place. Like the fact that his rival, Ted, got the promotion instead of him. Dick worries that Ted's promotion gives him a leg up with the girl of both men's dreams. Dick leaves feeling determined. He rushes to call Sally before Ted can. The tone in this instance should reflect Dick's upbeat point of view and competitive attitude toward the situation. If your romance is light and breezy, Dick views this obstacle as a fun challenge. He finds a way to woo Sally, no matter what comical lengths he must go to. If your romance is a tragedy, Dick views this scene as one more nail in his coffin.

⚡ You are writing a Thriller. Dick is at the company picnic in the park. The sky is overcast and threatening rain. The barbecue smoke makes his eyes water and nose run. He hates hotdogs. He hates his co-workers. He wishes he never had to see those drunken slobs ever again; but he grins and bears it until he can steal the research documents. So, he sips water. He smiles, nods, and bides his time. When he feels everyone is drunk enough, he goes back to the office and begins the search. In this example, Dick views the situation as dark and bleak. He focuses on the negative. The picnic is something to be endured to meet his goal.

🎭 You are writing a Literary novel. Dick is at the company picnic in the park. He desperately needs the promotion. He has child support and outrageous alimony to pay. He can't afford to be unemployed. The sun burns. He sweats profusely. The smoke is suffocating and the stench of roasting steak makes his stomach churn. Dick circulates. He shakes hands and fake smiles at his coworkers until his jaws hurt. He finds out Ted got the promotion. In fact, Dick's department is being cut. Dick is grateful when it starts raining so he can leave and drown his sorrows in a bottle of Scotch. In this example, the tone could be comic or tragic. The reader walks away, wryly acknowledging that bad things happen to good people; or, he walks away ruminating on the evils of cruel corporations.

Revision Tips

✍ As you read through your manuscript, consider the narrator's tone. Can you identify it? Do you want the story to be breezy, syrupy, gripping, horrifying, or funny?

✍ What is your genre? Does the tone correlate?

✍ Look at your descriptions and setting. How does the point of view character view the situation? Is it consistent with the tone you have adopted? Do the details that your character focuses on and the words he used to relate them support the tone?

✍ Is your tone consistent? Do you find yourself handling the material as melodramatic in one scene and comedic in another?

CHARACTER DESCRIPTION

Creative character descriptions are hard to master. There are long debates about how much character description is enough and how much is too much. Some readers want to know hair and eye color, height and weight, etc. Some want to fill in their own details. Not enough detail and you have talking heads. Too much and you turn some readers off. The choice is yours. Write what you enjoy reading. Either way, you have to define your character in a way that makes the reader care what happens to him.

The important thing about character description is keeping in mind the viewpoint lens filtering the information. If you are in Dick's head, self-description is tricky. Dick can compare and contrast himself to someone else. Someone can insult or praise Dick's appearance. Mirror gazing is considered cliché. The following descriptions are narrator intrusion in anything other than omniscient POV.

Dick's blue eyes lit up when he saw Sally.

This does not work if you are writing from Dick's point of view. Dick would not think "his blue eyes lit up." Sally could see his blue eyes light up. An omniscient narrator could say it. A first or third person narrator would not.

Dick stared at his handsome reflection in the dresser mirror. His eyes were blue. His nose was crooked. His chin was dimpled.

This is you, the author, telling us what Dick looked like.

Dick was a thirty-five-year-old with a pot belly and no hair.

Dick would not talk about himself that way. Another point of view character would be "talking to the audience" if he described Dick this way. Sally could describe Dick this way:

"Your nose looks like you head-butted a rhino, your big brown eyes are bloodshot, and that dimple doesn't make up for the weakness of your chin."

You need to give your reader a firm idea of who they are dealing with more so than the color of his eyes. Is Dick harsh and judgmental, sweet and lazy, or coarse and fun-loving? The reader fills in whether she thinks that person is corpulent or thin, attractive or not, based on the way the character comes across. It creates dissonance when a character's physical description counters what the reader feels about him. This is done accidentally or on purpose.

The character's voice, thoughts, and emotions say more about the character than facial features. The way the character thinks and feels about other people and the way he navigates the world illustrate the type of person he is. The reader fills in what she believes that type of person looks like based on her background and experience. Unless you specify the nationality, race, and sexual orientation of your character, a reader fills in those blanks to suit her own prejudices. Anglo-Saxon, heterosexual, English-speaking writers in North America tend to write with the assumption that their characters (and readers) are Anglo-Saxon, heterosexual, English-speakers unless otherwise specified. Humans are a bit egocentric that way. The delicacy is to not stereotype in an insulting way.

The assumption that everyone is like the writer is a plot hole. Don't assume everyone who reads your book shares your proclivities and demographics. Don't use the assumption of sameness as shorthand. It leaves some readers confused.

Unless a character's physical attributes affect the story in a prominent way, it is more important to tell the reader who the character is, or believes he is. If it is essential that Jane wears designer clothes and four-inch heels, tell us why. Designer clothes in Milan may not resemble designer clothes in Milwaukee. It is illogical to assume that all of your readers wear designer clothes and four-inch heels or that all of your readers are familiar with a certain section of New York City. This is one reason some of the Chick Lit novels set in New York or Los Angeles left readers in other demographics cold.

A reader unfamiliar with New York or Los Angeles society may view the characters as warped rather than endearing. Practical readers might think splurging on designer duds is stupid.

As outlined in Story Building Blocks II, it is useful to assign each main character a personality type. The traits propel them and affect the way other people see them. Temperament types are universal. This may sound like too much work, but it is well worth it to do the research. Personality types react to each other in different ways and your readers will not be the same temperament type.

A situation can cause Dick to view Sally in a different light. He might have a negative opinion of her at first and change his mind later. You can illustrate the shift in Dick's opinion of Sally through description.

First impression: Sally strode into the conference room. Her tight gray dress crackled like stiff paper. Her pale hair was clamped in a tight bun at the back of her head. She met his glance with cold, dark eyes and a clenched jaw. Dick straightened in his chair and ran a finger inside his collar. This witch would not be an easy sell.

Final impression: Sally slipped into the conference room. A tight navy dress hugged her curves. A few amber curls escaped a loosely gathered knot. Sally's flicker of a smile faded. Dick squirmed in his chair and ran a finger inside his collar. The memory of her glorious hair spread out across his bed made his skin prickle. He shuffled the papers in front of him. Sally had yet to sign on the dotted line, the tantalizing witch.

Personality clashes may cause Dick to view Sally in a negative light, even if she is runway model gorgeous. If Dick and Sally have a turbulent history, Dick thinks Sally's designer dress and shoes are an affectation rather than a turn on. These moments create tension.

Looks and personality are not synonymous. A character may not have symmetrical features or a svelte waistline, but she is lovely to know and a joy to be around. Her good nature makes her attractive to the viewer. A well-manicured, stately matron may have gutter sensibilities and a lewd sense of humor. Stereotypes are boring. Shake it up.

Characters project a false self to protect their inner child. An insecure person might make sure every hair is in place. A secure person might not care how she looks.

If Dick's socks don't match because he accidentally pulled a blue and a black sock out of the laundry basket, how secure he is determines whether he delivers a blistering counter-attack when Sally points it out or bursts into genuine laughter over the error. Make sure your characters are multi-dimensional.

Look for instances where your point of view character analyzes another character. How does he feel and react when that person is around? Is there a dichotomy between his reaction and how he should feel? Dissonance creates tension.

This revision layer does not require you to cut all descriptions of clothes, hair, and accoutrements. Rather, it asks you to take a fresh look at your descriptions and decide if they are meaningful and powerful rather than bland and boring.

Revision Tips

✍ Save a copy of your draft as "Character Descriptions" and delete everything but the character descriptions. You can highlight the descriptions on a printed draft if you prefer.

✍ Have you described the character as he enters the story?

✍ Are your descriptions meaningful and original or full of clichés and weak adjectives? Have you repeated the same information?

✍ Are there instances of dissonance?

✍ Do words and actions illustrate the character? Do they play against type?

✍ Is your point of view character's description of someone accurate or inaccurate due to his personality, past history, or current situation? Does his opinion change?

✍ Have you used clichés or purple prose?

DIALOGUE

Dialogue consists of statements, interjections, questions, answers, commands, and rebuttals. It provides point and counterpoint, heated arguments, persuasive arguments, and tender seduction. Dialogue accelerates the pace. If well written, it propels the reader swiftly onward. If poorly written, it slows the reader down to a crawl. You should avoid slowing the reader down at a time when they should be accelerating.

There are four parts to editing dialogue: formatting, dialogue tags, delivery, and content.

FORMATTING

Quotation Marks: I once picked up a book where the writer used hyphens instead of quotation marks. The formatting annoyed me, so I didn't purchase the book. Funky formatting slams on the breaks and may cost you readers. Your words, not your formatting, should have center stage. Quotation marks are invisible sentinels alerting the reader that someone is speaking. Readers sail past them without blinking.

When reviewing formatting, turn on **Reveal Codes** by clicking on the ¶ icon on the toolbar. It will highlight extra spaces and funky formatting.

Double quotation marks signify dialogue. A simple line of dialogue should look like this:

"No,"·I·said.

"No!"·I·said.

"No?"·I·asked.

Single quotation marks signify that you are repeating what someone else said. Quotes within quotes should appear in this order: an outer quotation mark, a single quotation mark, content, a single quotation mark, and an outer quotation mark. There are no spaces between the outer and inner quotation marks.

It should look like this: "'What you said.'"

Not this: "·'What you said.'·"

✎ **Em-dash:** Use an em-dash (—) to indicate an interruption or sudden change of thought. To insert an em-dash, click on [Insert] [Symbol] [More Symbols] [Special Characters], locate the em-dash, and hit Enter.

"What the —."

The em-dash is a specific ASCII character. Using automatic formatting to convert two dashes to the em-dash may not translate to E-book upload services.

🖊 **Ellipsis**: Use an ellipsis to show an unfinished thought, faltering speech, or trailing off. It is considered incorrect to use it solely to illustrate a pause in speech. To insert an ellipsis, click on [Insert] [Symbol] [More Symbols] [Special Characters], locate the ellipsis, and hit Enter.

"But ..."

An ellipsis is a specific ASCII character. It is not three, or four, or six periods in a row. Using automatic formatting to convert several periods into an ellipsis won't necessarily translate to E-book upload services.

An ellipsis indicates words (or entire sections) intentionally left out of a quote.

The boat capsized ... and the passengers were helicoptered out later that afternoon.

An ellipsis prefaces innuendo.

Dick smirked. "Would you like to inspect my ... package?"

A space follows the ellipsis if there are additional words or formatting after it. A period should follow the ellipsis at the end of a sentence.

"But, how you can you ... ?"

"I think so, I mean ...."

⊞ DIALOGUE TAGS

Whether you should use descriptive or adverb dialogue tags is hotly debated. Standard dialogue tags are *said* and *asked*. The mind skips over them, so they are considered invisible.

"Some editors don't mind a few creative tags," she posited.

"Some may allow adverb tags," she said skeptically.

"Adverb tags are generally frowned upon. Break this rule at your own peril," she said mischievously.

Creative tags are considered speed bumps that force the reader to decide if the dialogue agrees with the tag. You are supposed to show not tell. The creative tag is redundant if your dialogue has done its job properly. That said, not all readers mind an occasional creative tag as long as it isn't melodramatic. Some resources actually recommend them. Use them as you see fit and check for repetition. Cut them down to a few times per manuscript.

Creative tags include:

acknowledged	confessed	interrupted	restated
added	cried	laughed	retorted
admitted	croaked	lectured	revealed
advised	decided	lied	roared
agreed	declared	mentioned	ruled
alluded	demanded	moaned	sang
announced	denied	mumbled	scolded
answered	described	murmured	screamed
approved	dictated	muttered	screeched
argued	emphasized	nagged	shouted
asserted	estimated	neighed	shrieked
assumed	exclaimed	noted	sighed
assured	explained	notified	snapped
babbled	expressed	objected	snarled
bargained	expounded	observed	sneered
barked	feared	offered	snorted
began	giggled	pleaded	sobbed
begged	grinned	pointed out	spoke
bellowed	groaned	prayed	spouted
blustered	grunted	predicted	sputtered
boasted	gurgled	pouted	stammered
bragged	guffawed	promised	stated
brayed	hinted	questioned	stormed
cackled	hissed	reassured	stuttered
called	hollered	recalled	suggested
cawed	howled	reiterated	threatened
chattered	implied	related	thundered
choked	implored	remembered	uttered
claimed	indicated	repeated	vented
commanded	inquired	replied	vocalized
commented	insisted	requested	voiced
complained	instructed	responded	vowed

| wailed | whimpered | whispered | <u>yawned</u> |
| warned | whined | wondered | yelled |

Most editors would like you to avoid wriggling eyebrows, rolling eyes, and animal noises. You cannot bay, snort, guffaw, or laugh a word. You can utter a sentence between guffawing and laughing, but it should be an action tag. It cannot replace *said*. Words that need to be action tags are underlined above. See the section on clichés.

You don't need a tag with every line of dialogue, particularly if only two characters are talking. Insert a tag every three or four beats to remind the reader whose turn it is. The more characters you have exchanging dialogue, the more tags you have to use to cue the reader as to who is saying what.

Think about conversations at a party. A simple conversation involves two people. A triangular conversation involves three. More than three constitutes a complicated conversation. It's like playing jump rope. A character must decide when to cut in.

Characters interrupt and cut each other off, talk over each other, and finish each other's sentences. Some people stammer, stutter, or take a while to finish a sentence.

An alternative to creative and adverb tags is the action tag or action beat. The action tag shows the character doing something either prior to, in the middle of, or after the statement or question.

Your dialogue should look like one of these examples. Note the correct formatting. Commas, periods, and question marks should fall within the quotation marks (in American English). A comma separates the dialogue from the standard tag. A period separates the dialogue from an action tag. The same formatting for the standard tag applies to a creative tag.

No tag: "I see."

Standard tag in the front: Sherlock said, "I see."

Standard tag in the middle: "I see," Sherlock said. "I have been misinformed."

Standard tag at the end: "I see," Sherlock said. (or) "I see," said Sherlock.

Action tag in the front: Sherlock cleared his throat. "I see."

Action tag in the middle: "I see." Sherlock cleared his throat. "I was misinformed."

Action tag at the end: "I see." Sherlock cleared his throat.

Action combined with a standard tag: Sherlock pointed to the clock and said, "I must be off."

Revision Tips

✍ Proofreading for formatting errors is an essential final pass before you submit or upload your manuscript. Go over the manuscript three or four times with Reveal Codes ¶ on. Yes, it is irritating and boring. Do it anyway. Bribe someone else go over it with a fresh pair of eyes. If you self-publish, once you have the proof in your hands, proofread again. Do it with the second and third proofs. Do it until you have it perfected. The quotation marks, periods, spaces, and commas look like spinning ants after awhile, which makes them hard to catch.

✍ Are quotation marks, periods, and tags where they should be? Do you have extra spaces?

✍ Do a search [Control] [F] for ellipses by copying the ellipsis character into the search field. Highlight the ellipsis character, hit [Control] [C] for copy, place the cursor in the search field and hit [Control] [V] then Find All. Have you committed ellipsis abuse? Several times within a chapter is considered acceptable. Several times in a sentence is not.

✍ Do a search [Control] [F] for an em-dash by copying the em-dash character into the search field. Highlight the em-dash character, hit [Control] [C] for copy, put the cursor in the search field and hit [Control] [V] then Find All. Have you committed em-dash abuse? Several times within a chapter is considered acceptable. Several times in a sentence is not.

> ✍ Look over the draft at each passage of dialogue. Have you used creative dialogue tags to inform how the dialogue was delivered? Can you change it so the dialogue does the work?

🔳 DELIVERY

Each main character should have unique speech patterns, dialects, tics, or word choices. If they are all from the same small town and share the same ethnicity, they use the same slang, jargon, and colloquialisms. However, you can give each of them a unique voice through dialogue cues. Is Jane breathy and timid? Is Dick commanding and confident? Is Sally glib and sarcastic?

Dialogue cues express how the dialogue is delivered. They impart dialect, inflection, pacing, pattern, pitch, quality, tone, and word choice. Over ninety percent of communication is nonverbal. When editing your dialogue, how your character speaks and reacts is as important as what comes out of his mouth.

👤 **Cadence and word order:** Cadence is the rhythm of the words, the number of beats in a sentence, and the modulation of a voice. Cadence can be soothing, like a poem about sunshine, or intentionally jarring. Shakespeare and Dr. Seuss used iambic pentameter as cadence. Cadence is mixing long beats and short beats. Refer to the section on sentence structure for information on how to craft beats.

Cadence is obvious when you listen to foreigners speak. Spanish is staccato. German is guttural. French and Italian sound melodic and fluid. Japanese and Chinese sound high and nasal. Hindu and Urdu sound lower and nasal. Swedish and Norwegian sound high and bouncy.

English can be fast in New York and slow in New Orleans. A foreigner speaking English would use a different cadence than an American would.

In some languages the adjective comes after the word. Black cat in French is *le chat noir*. The statement "*I cannot dance*" in German is "*Ich tanzen nicht.*" The *nicht* has guttural emphasis and the modifier comes after the verb. A German unfamiliar with English might say *I dance not*. A Frenchman might say: *the problem impossible*. If you watch Agatha Christie's Poirot movies, actor David Suchet (a Brit) does an amazing job with the cadence of Poirot's Belgian-influenced English. Watching foreign films is a great way to learn a language's cadence.

Dialect: There are northern, southern, mid-western, east coast, and west coast dialects in the US. There are dialects in every country across the globe. Characters from Wales are almost indecipherable to those from London. Characters from Glasgow are indecipherable to those from Edinburgh.

The debate is whether to spell the dialect phonetically or not. This method was used liberally in the past. A modern reader struggles with Thomas Hardy's prose. Phonetic dialogue creates speed bumps. Used sparingly and judiciously, you might get away with it. Write all dialogue this way, and you lose a modern reader. It's much better to illustrate the dialect with cadence, word order, and inflection.

"I's got me som a dem melons."

It is better to write:

"I got me some of them melons."

Dialect is revealed through word choice and word order. It is more a reflection of education and exposure than demographics or geography. It doesn't matter if an educated character lives in New York or New Orleans. He may use colloquialisms, jargon, and slang, but he *speaks* properly. It is humorous when a character speaks properly then dumbs it down, or turns on the accent, for other characters. A character can attempt to influence someone by talking like him. He can do it to express contempt for another character.

Characters with limited education use limited vocabulary. They rely on slang and jargon more heavily. As a caution, dialect done poorly or stereotypically can be insulting. You risk alienating readers. You have to decide how sensitive or politically correct you want to be and whether the use of it serves a specific purpose.

Enunciation: Most characters desire to be understood and attempt to enunciate clearly most of the time. Some characters mumble, particularly teenage boys and small children. Mentally ill people can mumble. Dementia patients might mumble. Characters mumble to obscure their words when they don't want to say something or are ashamed of saying something. It is important to enunciate clearly when speaking to someone who has poor hearing or is unfamiliar with your language. Enunciation degrades when your characters are upset or angry. Characters run words together, skip over words, or leave words off. Characters over-enunciate when they are impatient, angry, or feel like they are talking to an idiot. Enunciation can display caring and empathy or anger and resentment.

🗣 **Inflection**: Inflection, or prosody, is the pitch of the voice. It is adding emphasis to words or word parts. An upward inflection at the end of a sentence implies hope or a question. A downward inflection at the end of a sentence implies doubt or a command. A character's voice is monotone and flat when he is bored. It is slow and low when he is depressed or sad. High-pitched and enthusiastic means he is happy or excited. If he speeds up and gets louder, he is angry or excited. High-pitch and slow speed indicates he doesn't believe what he is hearing. Whoever your character is talking to picks up on the inflection right away, especially if it is counter to the content.

If Dick is genuinely smiling when he says something on the telephone, the other person picks up on the inflection. When you smile, the soft palate at the back of your mouth rises and makes sound waves more fluid. Dick might be forcing himself to smile, either to sell someone something or to humor a dangerous person. If he is relaxed and smiling, the other person feels that he is warm, friendly, and receptive. Most characters are bad at faking it. They struggle to maintain a pleasant tone when they are furious, but the edge comes through.

How Dick stresses specific words changes what he is saying. If he is defensive, he emphasizes *would you:*

"What *would you* like me to do about it?"

It is antagonistic. If he genuinely cares, he would emphasize *like us*:

"What would you *like us* to do about it?"

If he is bored or does not care, he does not emphasize any of the words.

The way a character breathes affects his inflection. If stressed, he breathes shallowly. The more upset he grows, the faster he breathes until he hyperventilates. His vocal cords contract and make the pitch higher. There is a reason why we tell hysterical people to take a deep breath. Breathing deeply relaxes the vocal cords and allows Dick to say what he needs to say in a reasonable tone of voice. If Jane is confronting an incoherent toddler in the middle of a tantrum, Jane should ask the toddler to stop and breathe so he can clearly articulate his need or desire. If she yells and gives in to her temper, she escalates the problem. If she says, "Can you calm down so I can understand you?" it defuses the problem. The upset person or toddler above all wants to be heard.

Pacing: Some characters talk rapidly. Some characters drawl lazily. Characters speak faster when anxious or excited, hyperthyroid, in a hurry, short-tempered, or don't wish to have a particular conversation. They speak slower when they are relaxed, hypothyroid, or medicated. They are slowest when calming someone down, reasoning with him, or questioning his intelligence. If someone is angry, responding with anger fuels the flames. Speaking calmly and rationally should tamp it down. Unless the fact that Dick is calm makes Jane angrier.

Characters conversing in their native language speak quickly. They have to slow down for children, someone who does not understand their language, or people with hearing deficits.

Pattern: Speech patterns differ substantially between the educated and non-educated, among geographic locations, and within languages spoken. Trained listeners can identify a speaker's origins from his speech. An African or Asian brought up in the American south will not speak like an African or Asian brought up in London. Studies have proven that children are more wary of people who don't sound like them than they are of people who don't look like them. A computer-generated voice cannot exactly mimic a human voice, so the mechanical voice makes us anxious.

Pattern is expressed through syntax, or the way the character structures his sentences. It is choosing to offer a statement as a question or a declaration and the subsequent vocabulary choice. Changing the modifier after a statement from *absolutely* to *I think* or *do you think*, changes the meaning of the sentence from *I'm certain* to *I'm uncertain*.

"I want to go to France for vacation, don't you?"

"I want to go to France for vacation, I know you do too."

"Do you think we should go to France for vacation?"

"France is magnificent, don't you think?"

"France is truly magnificent, is it not?"

Pattern is expressed through morphology, the meaning of words used, and subject-verb agreement. It is referred meaning such as antonyms and synonyms. It is the connection of one word to another, such as *disk* to *disk player*. It is patterns of words within and across languages. It is the rules that govern the languages.

In English, the adjective precedes the noun: *the black cat*. In French, the adjective follows the noun: *the cat black*. In German, the negation comes after the verb: *I dance not*.

Patterns are expressed through phonology, which is the way a language sounds. The beats in American English are different from the beats used when speaking English in England or Ireland.

America: "Jerk! Why didn't you wait for me?"

England: "You should've waited, you silly bugger."

Ireland: "And you couldn't wait for me, could you, lad?"

Beats are covered more thoroughly in the sentence structure section.

Pattern is expressed through acoustics or phonetics. Acoustics is the way the sound resonates in the listener's ear. It is hard sounds versus soft sounds. Phonetics is the physical production of sound, like the placement of the tongue to roll R's, the nasal quality, the emphasis on consonants, and the way a word is broken up into syllables *i-di-ot* versus *i-diot*. It is the hiss of an *S* or whether a *C* sounds like an *S* (*certain*) or a *K* (*cash*).

Patterns can reveal state of mind or pathology. Characters that are confident use short, declarative sentences and offer precise answers. Characters that are confused or lying use long, rambling sentences and never really answer the question. Characters with antisocial psychiatric disorders, or disorders such as hysteria, have problems following a conversation or sticking to the point. They meander, lie, and change the topic.

🗣 **Pitch**: Pitch can indicate state of mind, gender, or age. Women and children tend to have high-pitched voices. Men tend to have deeper voices. I once knew a little girl with a very deep voice. It was hilarious. Men with higher-pitched voices are considered effeminate. Conversely, a woman with a deep or contralto voice is considered sexy. A deeper pitch can indicate aggressiveness when used by a male or female. We use a higher pitch when talking to babies, kittens, puppies, dimwits, and psychopaths. A deeper pitch can be Jane's attempt at sexiness. A higher pitch can mean Dick is mocking Sally.

🎤 **Tone**: We all recognize *the tone*, the one our mother adopts when she shouts our first and middle names, alerting us that we are in trouble. The tone your character uses to impart his word choice can overturn the meaning of the words. Dick saying, "*Now, Jane*," can be a warning, a tender jibe, or an angry deflection. Is Dick being frivolous or serious, casual or formal, sweet or stuffy?

A tone can be: bitter, casual, comic, controlled, elaborate, experimental, flat, frivolous, grave, humorous, impassioned, impersonal, ironic, light, loose, objective, offhand, ornate, personal, plainspoken, rambunctious, reasonable, reasoned, reserved, serious, simple, somber, subjective, sweet, vexed, or zany.

"With most of them, if you add *ly*, you have an adverb tag," she said frivolously.

Contractions are informal. If a character never uses contractions, he sounds stuffy or pompous. If you write a historical piece, the aristocracy or royalty may always speak formally.

🗣 **Vocabulary**: The more a character reads and exposes himself to the written word, the larger his vocabulary. The more he learns about through reading or higher education, the easier it is for him to express sophisticated thoughts. This does not mean his perspective on events is free from prejudice. This means he is more likely to express his thoughts eloquently and pull from resources to support his proposition or refute someone else's. He may have to limit his word choice when dealing with certain people. A character may be intellectually gifted but practically useless. A character may not be intellectually intelligent but extremely street smart.

🗣 **Word Choice**: Word choice says a lot about how your character feels about the topic, the person he is speaking to, and his mood. It speaks to his background and education level. It reveals whether he is confident or uncertain, diplomatic or insulting. A character may choose his words carefully, because he is afraid to offend. A character may blurt out whatever enters his head without filtering it.

📧 CONTENT

This brings us to content. Dialogue is not everyday conversation. Dialogue cuts out the boring bits and irrelevant information to hone in on the purpose for having the conversation. Dialogue should reveal, obscure, confuse, deflect, derail, demand, beg, placate, or anger.

If the reader skims the dialogue while thinking, *blah, blah, blah*, you have a plot hole. If you make the reader laugh out loud, or identify with the character or situation, you have him hooked. If your dialogue achieves something, it earns its page time.

In compelling dialogue, the course of conversation rarely flows smoothly. Characters talk about things they shouldn't, say things they don't mean, talk at crossed purposes, try to shout each other down, wheedle, plead, whine, gripe, mislead, and lie.

A conversation can bring a character down from a precipice of anger, frustration, depression, or jealousy. A friend can calm and soothe or bank the fires.

Use dialogue conflicts to illustrate your protagonist's progress toward and away from his goal. Use dialogue to create conflict at scene level. Use dialogue to reveal change.

A conversation can reveal character. What Dick chooses to say and what he avoids saying speaks volumes. It reveals whether he is patient and kind or brusque and cruel. A situation may force Dick to be brutal or brusque. How much he struggles with it tells us what kind of man he is.

You create conflict using dialogue in the following ways.

🐾 **Body language**: If what Dick says doesn't match his body language, Jane knows something is up. Smiling while sad and grinning while angry are sure signs that something is amiss. It may alert Jane that Dick is lying. Jane may change tactics or attempt to understand why Dick is sad or mad. She can ignore the underlying body language or be distracted and not notice it. Her inattention creates a bigger problem.

🐾 **Distractions:** If Dick talks to Jane while she is in the middle of something, like trying to write a chapter before the inspiration fades, Jane might hear Dick without really listening. She may say things like, "*Yeah, whatever*," or "*Sure, go ahead*." Because Jane didn't really attend to what she was agreeing to, there is conflict. Distractions can be physical, mental, or emotional. If Dick is watching an important football play on TV, he might ignore Jane. Jane may get mad. She may get even. Dick may miss the fact that Jane just said she was leaving him for the cabana boy.

🐾 **Jargon**: Different cultures use different words to describe things. If Dick jets off to London he might think "*Bobby*" is a person and "*shag*" is a carpet. He might be embarrassed when someone orders a "*spotted dick with cream*." All kinds of delightful (and tragic) mistakes can occur.

🐾 **Language**: If Dick is forced to deal with people who don't speak his language, he resorts to the basics: hand gestures, facial expressions, and sharing one word at a time. Misunderstandings are inevitable.

🐾 **Mars/Venus**: Dick and Jane have different conversational "currency." Men tend to report and feel they are supposed to take action. Women tend to relate anecdotes and want validation. Conflict ensues if they don't get what they want or need. Temperament type defies this stereotype.

Some temperament types want facts; others want impressions. Both could be male or female.

🗨 **One-up**: Dick and Jane's conversation can derail in a hurry if each is determined to come out on top or get the last word in. A couple in a power struggle can lob, parry, and zing in an escalating war that ruins a play, a concert, or a business dinner. The verbal war could serve as a distraction. Things are often said in the heat of the moment that they can't take back. Dick may need to grovel awhile to get back into Jane's good graces. Escalating one-up fights can illustrate the demise of a relationship gone wrong or make the scene goal impossible to accomplish.

🗨 **Repartee**: In a good conversation, Sally and Jane take turns. It's like watching a tennis match's serve and return. The pace can be intense, fast paced, and angry. It can be slow, witty, and fun. Sally can run on and on and never give Jane a chance to comment. Jane can be brusque and abrasive and cut Sally off every time she tries to say something. In real life, people interrupt and talk over top of one other. Groups divide into separate conversations, which can be fun if Jane misses something she should have been listening to. She may strive to listen to one conversation while carrying on another.

🗨 **Repetition**: Dialogue can be a plant and payoff used several times throughout a story to reveal change. The same statement, phrase, or question repeats but offers a different meaning each time. It can be humorous, poignant, uplifting, or gut wrenching. Use one plant and payoff phrase per manuscript for maximum impact.

🐾 **Too much information**: How open people are about themselves and their lives varies with each culture. Some characters tell people everything about anything. They have no problem talking about how much money they have or spend. They think everyone is interested in the cute things their toddler said. Their closet doors are wide open. Other cultures are more reserved. Their closet doors are slightly ajar or firmly closed. How much is too much varies within cultures. Even within a close group, there are differences in how comfortable characters are with sharing personal information. Someone carrying around shame is less likely to want broadcast his life story. Someone with a secret won't divulge much. Someone with poor boundaries will blurt out inappropriate details and turn people away. Put opposite characters together and you have an uncomfortable conversation.

🐾 **Witnessing**: Everyone wants to feel "heard." I would call that a basic human need. If Dick feels unheard, he may become angry and lash out. He may become depressed and withdraw. Either way, the scene goal is a bust or a success, depending on the intention.

Revision Tips

✍ Dialogue should serve a specific purpose, not act as filler. It should contain tension. Review the dialogue in each scene on the screen or in the printed draft.

✍ First look at the content. Is the dialogue performing a specific function or acting as filler?

✍ Do the lobs and parries follow a logical sequence? Because Jane said X, Dick said Y, which leads to Z. Are they deliberately not following the script?

✍ Nonverbal cues are as important as what is said and how it is said. Have you used nonverbal cues judiciously? They should give emphasis, not appear after every line of dialogue. You don't need to show reactions to every word spoken. Save physical responses and reactions for important revelations.

✍ Does each main character sound unique? Assign them a style then make sure his bits of dialogue are consistent. A character changes what he says and how he says it during intense conflict. Otherwise, he reverts to form.

✍ Choose words carefully. Make them fit the situation and the character. If they don't, cut them or change them. Use strong word choices to avoid passive or clichéd responses and weak dialogue.

INTERIORITY

Interiority refers to a character's inner life: his thoughts, feelings, and view of the world. In order to show interiority, you have to reveal to the reader your character's internal struggle and self-talk. What he says to himself affects what he does and says to others. Does internal monologue constitute telling? It shouldn't. Sometimes action and dialogue are not enough. We want to see inside Jane's head.

Interiority gives us insight into the character's thought processes, decision-making, internal struggle to do the right (or wrong) thing, his moral compass, and value judgments. It reveals how he perceives other characters, the overall story problem, and his internal dilemma.

Interiority is related via interior or internal thoughts, aka interior or internal monologue, aka internal narration. If the character argues with himself or talks to himself, it is interior or internal dialogue.

Characters don't normally think in full sentences or use big words. They say, "*Crap, that hurt!*" instead of "*Oh dear, my shin bumping into that chair was truly painful.*" They don't use proper grammar. Thoughts dart and are incomplete. However, rules that apply to dialogue also apply to internal dialogue and narration. Cut out the boring parts, give it something to do, and make it readable. It is important to use this device for effect and not to take up space. You can show a character struggling with what to do at a critical point. We don't need to read every single thought he has from minute to minute. He doesn't have to express a thought after every word spoken or action taken.

Interior monologue, or narration, is related in first person or close third person, unless you are using omniscient point of view. A character thinks in present tense, not past tense.

Dick would not think: Jane had only agreed to humor me. She had no intention of ever going through with it.

Dick would think: Jane is humoring me. She has no intention of going through with it.

Dick would not think of himself in third person: He couldn't go on. It was not possible.

Dick would think: I can't go on. It isn't possible.

Internal thoughts and narration do not require quotation marks. It is debatable whether internal dialogue should be italicized or underlined. Style guides insist that italicizing internal thoughts is the same as putting speech in quotation marks.

A rule that begs to be broken is that internal dialogue should be written in first person, present tense.

Dick walked down the hallway that smelled of disinfectant. *I hate this place*, he thought.

Some readers find the switch in tense annoying if the story is written in third person. It can take them out of the total immersion experience.

Third person without offset: Dick walked down the hallway that smelled of disinfectant. He hated the place.

Third person with italics: Dick left the conference room. *I really blew it*, he thought to himself. *What now?*

Third person with quotation marks: "I really blew it," Dick said to himself as he left the conference room. "What now?"

Third person close up: Dick left the conference room. *I blew it. What now?*

Narration first person: I walked down the sidewalk feeling a twinge of disgust. I really blew it.

Narration third person tense switched: Dick followed the sidewalk feeling a twinge of disgust. *I really blew it,* he thought.

Narration third person tense not switched: Dick followed the sidewalk. He had blown it and it disgusted him.

It is up to you whether you choose to relate thoughts as internal dialogue or internal thoughts and narration. As a rule, talking to oneself with quotation marks is a speed bump that rewording into internal thought or narrative removes.

Dick rubbed his face. His eyes were dry. His limbs were heavy. He had to stay awake. There would be plenty of time to sleep after the crime was solved.

You can ramble for sentences while using third or first person describing thoughts without formatting or italics and get away with it as long as you are focusing on the point of view character for that scene. Internal narration remains the tense in which you are writing, which is usually past tense.

Incorrect: Sally is lying. Dick senses it.

Incorrect: Sally was lying. Dick senses it.

Correct: Sally was lying. Dick sensed it.

Use internal narration to reveal things the character can't say but wants to, undermine the words coming out of his mouth, or to express his true feelings.

Internal narration can be used in small doses to reveal backstory.

"No, I can't go with you," Jane said. Because if I went with you, I couldn't bear to return, then where would I be?

"Of course, I'd love to." Sally smiled. I'd love to wring your wretched neck.

"I see," Dick said. It was suddenly clear that she had been lying to him for months, perhaps years. What had she said last summer? Oh, yes, "Sometimes you have to leave to stay." And the summer before that, when she left for a girls' weekend in Frisco, had she been with her friends or her lover? Dick's fist curled, but he kept his arm down. Gentlemen never hit ladies, even if they weren't acting like ladies, even if they were cutting your heart out while you were still conscious.

Revision Tips

✍ Mark the places where you have used internal narration or dialogue. Is it formatted consistently?

✍ Is there more internal dialogue than dialogue? If so, consider reducing it or turning it into dialogue between characters.

✍ Does the internal narration serve a useful purpose? If not, change it or cut it.

✍ Does a single passage ramble on too long and interrupt the flow? If so, trim it.

✍ Have you been consistent with verb tense and point of view?

BODY LANGUAGE

There are a few cardinal sins in terms of body language. The first is when disembodied body parts do things. Eyes do not roll, drop, run, scan, or travel. They cannot be glued or pasted. A gaze can be fixed. A gaze can travel. A heart cannot drop. It can beat hard. It can thump. It can't literally travel up your throat.

Incorrect: Her fingers clenched.

Correct: She clenched her fingers.

Incorrect: His nose wrinkled.

Correct: He wrinkled his nose.

The problem occurs when we try to cut out excessive pronouns by having the body part perform the action. I was guilty of this until an editor pointed it out at a conference. My hand slapped my forehead, which brings us to the second cardinal sin: clichés.

The third cardinal sin is use of the same dull, repetitive body movements. We all cry, laugh, run, sit, stand, and walk. It's okay to have your characters do these simple movements sometimes. Some editors think these words are invisible, like *said* and *asked*. Others want you to change it up. Write the way you want. The important thing is to avoid clichés, purple prose, and repeating the same word too frequently on the page.

The key is to combine body language with interiority, actions, and words with mindfulness and purpose. If you show over-reaction to every single stimulus, it is overkill. Make sure that body language corresponds to, or contradicts, the emotion expressed for a reason. Thoughts and actions should not duplicate dialogue. Don't show a character feeling angry, tell us he is angry with an adverb tag, and have him shout all in the same sentence. Readers get it the first time.

Utilizing responses in an intentional way takes your work from bland to brilliant. It wastes time to perfect the first draft. As you write, throw in whatever standard crutches your brain reaches for. Write down enough that you have the intention of the scene. Dick has a fight. Dick sits or stands. He laughs, coughs, or frowns.

Write clichés and purple prose if it is what you normally throw in. Use the revision layer to rework the passages. Zoom your verbal camera in close to take in small details where it is most important. Widen the verbal camera's focus when you relate scenes of lesser importance. Continuous, play by play, in-depth detail makes your prose exhausting.

Choose the sections you want to highlight judiciously and keep the verbal camera zooming in and out. Give your reader a satisfying ride. Don't stay focused for too long in any one spot. Don't zoom in on unessential details. When you have action and reaction in a scene, examine it carefully. What should you add, keep, or cut?

Peruse your manuscript. Highlight the critical encounter in each scene. Every scene should have a setup, a conflict, and a resolution that leads to a new conflict. You should have three or four key turning points in the overall story. Those scenes deserve the most attention. There will be three or four minor turning points. They deserve some attention. There will be lighter moments that require little detail. The rest are subtler conflicts that require the barest attention to detail.

At any given moment, characters do multiple things. They think, feel, move, and/or speak. Each item brings something slightly different to the picture. Jane may feel angry, but force herself to speak calmly. Dick may play checkers with his child while worrying about work the next day or listening to a conversation Jane is having in the next room.

Not every encounter needs to reveal every beat. Use more beats when the tension is high, less when the tension is low. Use extreme actions and reactions sparingly. The verbal camera should zoom in on the mechanics during critical parts and zoom out for the noncritical parts.

Make sure you relate the beats in a logical order.

#1. The brain receives the stimulus. A stimulus is triggered by the senses. It can be something your character hears, intuits, sees, smells, tastes, or touches.

#2. The body has an involuntary response that takes a nanosecond. The limbic system evaluates the stimulus and sends chemicals racing through the body as neurons fire, depending on its evaluation of whether the stimulus is negative, positive, or neutral. The brain decides instantaneously if there is a potential threat or reward.

#3. The response triggers a reflexive action.

#4. The brain then regains control over the body and makes a conscious decision about how to proceed.

A posited theory is that everyone we meet (and everything we come across) leaves a neural imprint. The brain decides if a person, place, or thing is a friend or foe and whether the next encounter will be negative or positive. The composite images are stored in an easily accessed file folder for comparison. How much a person or thing resembles the positive or negative composites determines how likely you are to like or dislike a new person, place, or thing when you encounter it. It decides whether snakes are lovely or lethal, whether a physical action is comforting or threatening, and whether an action you take is likely to result in reward or punishment.

It compares faces and decides that your new boss looks a lot like the girl you liked in elementary school. Your initial reaction is positive. She may turn out to be perfectly awful.

The brain makes these split-second decisions every second of every day. It is important to understand this process as you write, but it's only necessary to zero in on this part of the response at the most critical turning points of your story.

Next, the body reacts involuntarily to the stimulus. It recoils or reaches out. It startles or is soothed. A character gasps, coughs, sneezes, laughs, or screams. This reaction is embedded deep within the animal part of the brain. It is governed by sheer instinct and raw emotion. It is the fight or flight response at play. His pulse, breathing, and muscles react. His skin erupts in chills. His mouth goes dry. The character is not speaking or moving yet. He flinches, blinks, tenses, and displays a micro-expression.

What happens next depends on how the brain filters the stimulus through the character's conditioning, personality, and emotional connection to the stimulus. It tests the emotion of the moment. The brain decides to override or reinforce the initial involuntary response. If the stimulus is a threat from a comforting person, it causes dissonance. The same is true if the loving gesture is issued from a threatening stimulus. Dick's impulse may be to hug someone. It is awkward when that someone pulls away from it.

Finally, the character's conscious mind takes over and is free to decide which course of action to take next. The body recovers from the initial reflex. It overcomes the muscle memory and moves with intention. Conscious control over his breathing, pulse, and muscles is restored. Dick moves deliberately forward or backward and speaks. He alters his breathing, flexes his trembling knees, or relaxes his tightened gut and jaw. He smiles and shakes hands or fake smiles and avoids shaking hands.

If Dick has been startled, shocked, or wounded, his body recovers. Writers often forget to mention this step of the process. His system returns to normal once the threat has passed. Make sure you show the recovery after a major impact.

Cuddling, kissing, and hugging are often signs of affection. They could be signs of aggression if the character receiving the affection doesn't want it. There are situations in which a character must control involuntary responses, especially if Dick is a spy, a cop, or pretending to be someone he isn't. If faced with an angry mugger or screaming toddler, Dick's initial primordial response might be recoil. His body might tense to strike. If it is a mugger, he lets the punch fly, unless the mugger is holding a gun pointed at his head. If it is a toddler, Dick overrides the urge to strike and deals with it another way. Unless, he has poor self-control or the child is demon-possessed.

A few things to look for:

👁 Distance and Touching

Every character has a different idea of how close is close enough when speaking to other people. We call it personal space. It's uncomfortable when someone stands too close. It is crossing a psychological boundary. Some characters are touchy-feely types. An extrovert is more likely to be a hands-on kind of guy. An introvert hates being touched by people he doesn't know very well. A character who has been abused may not want anyone to touch him, no matter the reason, loving or otherwise. Some families and cultures are big on physical displays of affection, others aren't. A character might hug every one he has ever met upon seeing them again. Others prefer a handshake or a bow. The reasons can be personality, culture, or life experience.

Touch denotes a degree of intimacy. Someone touching Dick's shoulder could mean multiple things: desire, anger, or compassion. Little kids touch more than adults. A toddler is not self-conscious about where his hands land or where his head rests. The elderly can crave touch as much as toddlers. It may be decades since someone has hugged them or held their hand.

Jane might not mind being touched by a lover or best friend. She might object to being handled by a stranger at a party. Friends and family touch Jane to greet her, tease her, get her attention, help her, or hinder her. How comfortable she is with them makes a difference in how well she tolerates it.

Jane may normally love being touched by her husband, until she is angry with him. How your character feels affects how she processes the touch and the person touching her.

There are times when someone we don't know very well needs to touch us: massage therapists, hairdressers, doctors, nurses, medical personnel, rescue personnel, etc. A teacher may have to touch a child to direct him. A guard may have to touch Jane to direct her. It may make the character very uncomfortable. Children involved in sports are used to being tackled, patted, or punched by teammates. Others aren't.

Characters that are deceptive, don't like themselves, or are ashamed of something may avoid touch. They are uncomfortable when someone approaches them, pats them on the back, or moves in for a hug. Pedophiles touch inappropriately.

When a person touches Jane and it feels off, it sends a frisson of alarm through her system. Depending on the circumstances, Jane may subconsciously recoil, but consciously blow it off and make excuses for it. However, her subconscious remains on high alert until the danger has passed.

When describing touch in your fiction, make sure it is appropriate for the circumstances. Make sure you tell the reader how the character feels about being touched. Is it a good thing or a bad thing? What kind of caress, hug, or handshake was it? Is Jane's instinctive response to pull away when she knows she has to endure the hug? These small conflicts illustrate character, reveal relationships, and make characters very uncomfortable at scene level. Touch ignites an involuntary response, followed by a voluntary response, followed by a recovery. Illustrate the beats during critical encounters. The how and why are important. Was the touch appropriate or inappropriate? Tolerated or defended? Welcome or unwelcome?

Facial Expressions

There are myriad muscles that control the brow, chin, eyes, jaw, nose, and mouth. Some people can wiggle their ears. Different cultures utilize different expressions. Looking away may be deceptive in America, but indicative of respect in Japan. The important part when revising for body language is to note when and how you relate facial expressions and to avoid repetition and purple prose. One should not wriggle one's eyebrows while leering.

A character cannot control fleeting micro-expressions, the initial emotional response, but he quickly recovers from them. Facial expressions reflect our feelings about what is done and said, sometimes more eloquently or more obviously than we intend. Someone told me that there were only two true emotions: fear and love (or pleasure and pain). All other expressions stem from those two. The micro-expression field of study acknowledges seven. Love isn't one of them.

Unless the character is a professional interrogator, he is not going to hook Dick up to a lie detector, register his body heat and pulse, or measure the dilation of his pupils. There are, however, emotional triggers and signs that humans register in the space of a second. Most of your characters aren't trained to recognize them.

If you pay attention to what is happening in the body when a heightened emotion is experienced, you can make your characters believable. Highlight the places in your manuscript where you discuss emotions. Take a careful look at the choreography and word choices.

Anger: The jaw clenches. The lips thin and lift in a snarl. The nostrils flare. The eyebrows draw together. Aggression is a response to fear or a response to boundary violations. When Dick is angry, he may puff himself up to appear larger and stare his opponent into submission. His brow furrows. His blood pressure rises. The stress triggers a neurochemical cocktail in response to the fight or flight instinct. He flushes and clenches his fists. His sweat glands kick in. His muscles are primed to strike. He may shake his fist or point his finger. He may drift forward slightly, or step forward deliberately, depending on how much of a threat the opponent represents. His tone either lowers in warning or rises, depending on the circumstances. His anger may continue to simmer after the altercation. He usually vents to other people or indulges in a physical action to release it.

Anger can be expressed passively. After the initial response of jaw, nose, and lips, Jane may turn silent and look away. She may mutter under her breath or fake smile. She has the same physiological response, but her conscious instinct is to hide it. Passive people who are angry often cry when furious. As her throat closes and her blood boils, she becomes incoherent. She goes into wait and watch mode. Her anger simmers but she holds onto it. She is more likely to gossip and indirectly sabotage the person she is angry with. Temperament plays a role in how anger is expressed.

Contempt: A corner of the lip tightens and lifts. Contempt is in response to an intellectual boundary violation. Dick may make scornful or sarcastic comments. He may consciously override his initial response in an attempt to hide his disdain. He could state his true feelings in the matter. Contempt is in response to something or someone he does not believe, agree with, or like. He may deny his contempt, but his face betrays him.

Disgust: The nostrils clench and upper lip lifts. Dick may frown and pull back. He may flinch or purse his lips. He may utter exclamations of disgust in response. His heart rate slows. Disgust is in response to something he fears or abhors at gut level. His body retracts. He may put out his hand or wave someone away.

Fear: The upper lids and eyebrows lift. The lips stretch wide and pupils dilate. Fear is in response to a physical or emotional violation. Dick can react with mild fear or outright terror, depending on the stimulus. His response is instantaneous and involuntary. Dick's senses go on high alert. His fight or flight response is triggered. He either freezes or retracts. He may gasp. His muscles prepare to escape or avoid. He sweats. He shivers. The hair shafts stiffen. His pulse rate increases. He may go into shock, depending on the stimulus. His flesh may feel cold as the blood rushes to prime the muscles in his hands and legs and fuels the brain. He may step back or turn to run. He may cover his face and head with his arms. The rush of neurochemicals leaves him feeling shaky after the stimulus is dealt with.

Happiness: The corners of the lips lift, the teeth may show. The cheeks plump. The muscles around the eyes are engaged and wrinkles appear. The eyes may widen, or narrow if the nose wrinkles. Jane's posture relaxes and expands. She moves toward someone or something. Her body language is expansive. Neurochemicals induce a high. She may laugh. She is verbal and inclined to touch. She may be mildly delighted or completely overjoyed. Her focus may broaden to take in others. She wants to share her feeling.

Sadness: Pupils narrow. Upper eyelids droop. Corners of lips turn down. Sadness is a response to loss or hurt feelings. Jane's body language closes in protectively. She may cross her arms, lower her head, or turn away. She may grow quiet and have trouble speaking. Her throat feels constricted. Her eyes and nose prickle and water. Her chest feels heavy. She may become more aware of her pulse and breathing. A strong stimulus can feel like a blow to the viscera. She may gasp, cover her abdomen, or bend over. She may transition to shock. Sadness may be followed quickly by anger. With extreme grief, she may scream or yell. Her body may crumple to the floor. She holds herself and rocks back and forth. Crying can be soft and silent or guttural and loud. It can pass quickly or go on for minutes. The initial blast may be followed by softer gushes as Jane calms down.

👁 **Surprise**: The eyebrows lift and eyes open wide. The forehead furrows. Surprise can be a response to something positive, negative, or neutral. Jane can have a quick startle or a longer shock wave. The reaction can be followed immediately by fear, joy, or confusion. Depending on the stimulus, the jaw drops. Surprise is usually quick and over, but the stimulus sometimes makes Jane ruminate on it for some time. She may share her surprise with others in an attempt to understand it.

👁 Gestures

People "talk with their hands." Gestures are not random. They have purpose. They illustrate. They convey the words we do not speak. They confirm, deny, or emphasize what we say. Gestures vary from person to person and culture to culture. People can have nervous ticks. They can have "tells" that indicate they are lying, anxious, or unhappy. Use gestures wisely.

If a gesture begins before the words, it is a sign of honesty. If a gesture lags after the words, it's considered a sign of dishonesty. A gesture can be involuntary but squelched by the character. This is especially true if he is angry with someone he cares about or fears.

Gestures include:

air kisses
averted gaze
bared teeth
biting cuticles, hair, lips, or nails
blowing raspberries
bowing
chewing inside of lips or cheek
crossing ankles
crossing/uncrossing arms
crossing/uncrossing legs
curtsey
cuticle picking
elbow bump
eye rolling (or eyeball rotating)
eyebrows lift
eyebrows wrinkle
finger curling
finger pointing
fist shaking
fist swinging
flapping hands
flicking fingernails
fingernail tapping

genuflecting
grasping elbows
gripping hands
hands behind back
hands over face
hands over heart
hands together
hands wide
hat tip
index finger raised
kowtow
lip curls or purses
looking down
looking up
looking to the side
lowering arms
lowering hands
middle finger raised
mooning
mouth purses
mouth tightens
nodding
nose thumbing
nose wrinkles
pointing
pouting
raising arms in the air

rubbing earlobe
rubbing fingers
rubbing hands
scratching
scratching chin, ear, nose, or throat
shaking head
shrugging
sneering
sticking out tongue
swinging legs
slash throat with hand
smoothing hair
tapping fingers or toes
tucking legs under
thumbs up
thumbs down
thumb to the side
tightening fist
tugging clothes
tugging an ear
tugging hair
saluting
sweeping hands
waving

👁 Eye contact

Eye contact conveys interest and connection. Eyes express admiration, disbelief, and anger. Refusing eye contact means your character is angry, sad, guilty, or embarrassed. Breaking eye contact can signal it is someone else's turn to talk. Good eye contact is a general indicator of self-esteem. Staring is considered rude. Staring at a cat is an act of aggression.

Normal eye contact for one culture could be considered rude to another. Lowering one's eyes can be a sign of respect in some parts of the world. Make sure you utilize gestures appropriately, particularly when writing about other cultures. Do your research. If you are making up a completely new word, decide what the normal parameters are and keep it consistent.

👁 Lying

The practice of identifying liars has become an art as well as a science. There are multitudes of books, reams of research, and several television shows based on it. Dr. Paul Eckman's work is well worth reading. The show *Lie to Me* is well worth watching to learn more.

Whether someone is lying or honest is broadly characterized by how expansive or contractive his body language is. There may be master criminals, soulless sociopaths, trained spies, or sage sleuths who can outsmart everyone. For the rest, the normal rules governing behavior apply.

Someone who is telling the truth goes on the offensive. He is forward moving, expansive, broad gesturing, and offers distinct answers with *I* and *me*. He meets your gaze full on. His body gravitates toward yours in an attempt to be seen and understood and to connect. He gives the right amount of detail. He discusses the situation until you believe him. His story is explicit and consistent. He may be angry at being falsely accused, or having his honor questioned, but he does not feel guilty. He mirrors your posture. He talks expansively with his hands, starting the gesture before the words. He is relaxed and his smile engages other facial muscles. He points to himself and places his open hand on his chest. He is not afraid of close scrutiny.

The exception is when an honest person grows anxious when he isn't believed, especially in a situation where he feels unsafe. The situation may trigger anxiety responses just as in someone who isn't honest. He may flush with fury. A character that has an itch somewhere it's inappropriate to scratch isn't necessarily being deceptive. His underwear may not be where it belongs, or he may have a health problem that makes him itch everywhere. There are illnesses that trigger lip biting. Those gestures alone are not proof that someone is lying.

Someone who is lying goes on the defensive. He retracts and caves inward. He forces the gesture after the words. He rambles and mumbles and doesn't give direct answers. His smile never reaches his eyes. He gives shorter answers and changes the topic. He rarely uses *I* and *me*. His information is inconsistent. He averts his gaze. He may withhold details or gush with too much detail. It's more in the quality of what he says and what he didn't say. He answers a question with a question. He wants to escape the interrogation as soon as possible. His voice pitch rises because he is anxious. He blinks, licks his lips, and maintains poor eye contact. He gestures with palms up in a plea.

He may rub or scratch his nose, neck, or jaw. The stress makes him itch, sweat, and flush. He may stammer and mess up his words. He may hold his head still. His limbs feel wooden. He may lean forward, resting his elbows on a table or his knees, anything to make his body smaller. He places a barrier between you. He may slide an object between you or step behind a chair. Liars often say *honestly*, *believe me*, or *I'm telling the truth*. He may be smiling, but inside he is sweating. His brain races to come up with the details it lacks in answer to your questions. It is said that a liar doesn't memorize the story backwards, so asking him to repeat the information regressively trips him up.

For example, Dick asks Jane where she has been all day. She replies that she went to the hairdressers, the department store, Starbucks for a coffee, to the mall, and finally the grocery store. This answer displays the too much information rule. Most women would say, "*I had my hair done and went shopping.*" If Dick asks questions like, "*So, when did you go to Starbucks?*" Jane has to think hard about what she just made up. Did she say she stopped at Starbucks before or after department store? If your teen gives you a list, ask him to repeat it backwards. I bet he can't.

Jane might give Dick a long list if he makes the mistake of saying, "*So, what have you done all day?*" Those are fighting words and Jane may respond with a laundry list of the household chores, child-centered activities, and errands she accomplished in the space of eight hours punctuated by slamming drawers or cabinet doors, and a tone that drips acid. She isn't lying.

Revision Tips

✍ Examine each scene carefully. Highlight all instances of body language. Are the characters' actions and reactions in a logical order? Do they fit the circumstances?

✍ Have you zeroed in on the critical moments and panned the less critical moments?

✍ Have you used clichés or purple prose?

✍ Have you varied body language words or used the same simple words over and over? Have you repeated the same word too many times in a sentence or paragraph?

✍ In your story world, family dynamic, or culture, how is touch perceived? How close is too close? Do people hug, bow, or shake hands? Does a couple prefer to sit side by side or face to face?

✍ How comfortable is your character with physical interaction? How comfortable is she in her own skin? How affectionate or withdrawn is she?

✍ How did you express the emotional moments? Does the emotion fit the body language?

Diana Hurwitz

PERSUASION PLOT HOLES

At some point in your story, one character must convince another character of something or persuade him to do something. A frequent plot hole is when a character agrees to something or accepts something *because the plot called for it.* There is no rational discourse that shows the character being persuaded. I explored in Story Building Blocks II how the different temperaments process information, who they believe, and who they talk to. Their temperament affects which persuasion techniques work best with them.

The persuasion plot hole goes like this:

Dick hates the ocean. He hates the smell of it and the movement of it. He would never, ever, in his wildest dreams agree to go out on a boat, in the middle of the night, with a complete stranger. Miraculously, in Chapter Ten, he does just that because a blonde bombshell says, "*Let's take a ride.*" Dick might be tempted to do something in expectation of sexual favors. However, a rational human being would never go on a midnight cruise with a total stranger into a vast body of water where no one will ever know he has disappeared based

119

on a loose assumption of fleeting gain. Unless, it is the only way he can rescue someone he is deeply in love with, the only way to catch the drug lord at his game, or because the bombshell has a gun. Even then, it takes some convincing. Why should he trust this person?

There is a saying that you always have a choice unless you have a gun pointed at your head. I would argue this further. If someone has a gun pointed at your head, you actually have three choices. You can call his bluff. You can fight back and hope he is a crappy shot. You can believe that dying is a better alternative to doing whatever he wants you to do.

Persuasion is an art form. Toddlers learn it early. They widen their eyes, brighten their smiles, and ask, "*Pretty please?*" They hammer you with, "*Why?*" They stun you with the logic of, "*But I don't want to.*" Your characters are much the same when they attempt to persuade or dissuade another character.

Characters follow certain patterns. They are more likely to believe someone they like. They are more likely to support ideas that fall in line with their own. Some worry about what other people think, especially people they admire or look up to. They are more willing to trust someone who sounds the same as them over someone who looks the same as them.

Some characters look to other people when they aren't certain. Some respect authority, though what constitutes authority is variable. Characters accept an authority or sources they agree with over ones they don't. Some expect people to keep their word and finish what they start. They value that which is rare.

The situation and temperaments dictate which persuasion tactics are used and whether they are successful. The value of the objective determines how intensely a character fights for his side.

There are multiple persuasion techniques to employ.

☛ **Ask for more**: If Dick wants something, he can start off intentionally asking for too much so he can settle for something in the middle. This makes him seem like a reasonable kind of guy, except the part where he manipulated Jane by asking her do something she'd never allow to get her to agree to something she mildly objected to. Children are masters of this technique.

☛ **Appeal to authority**: Dick may be getting nowhere in his conversation with Jane. He can play the authority card. The authority can be real or imagined. "*They say*" is so random. Who are *they*? "*Authorities on the subject state ...,*" who are the *authorities*? Jane won't have time to verify them. Adding jargon and psychobabble gives his argument more power. Dick can flip this tactic and discount he authority Jane uses to support her argument. He can press her to come up with an answer as to who *they* are. He can refute the validity of the authority.

☛ **Assume concession**: Dick can circle around the point he is trying to make or the consensus is he trying to achieve.

He can talk at crossed purposes and end the conversation with, "*Well, I'm glad we all agree then.*" Except, Jane didn't agree. The comment makes her doubt herself. Did she agree? Maybe she did. If Dick pushes on in a confident manner, Jane may be bluffed into silence.

Attack the posse: Dick can tear down Jane's objectives by attacking the basis for her assumptions. He can attack her friends, her coworkers, her group members, or the social, political, or religious body as a whole. He can deride her documents or the source of her information. Jane is derailed into defending herself as apart from the group or into defending actions by the group she does not agree with. She is sidelined into defending her source rather than her point.

Baffle them with bull: If Jane seems unconvinced, Dick can bring in random and completely unrelated evidence to bolster his argument. Jane is forced to respond to each unrelated thread, rather than arguing the main point. Dick can sum up his argument as if everything he just said supported it. Jane is either confused enough to give in or calls him on it.

Bait and switch: Dick wants to achieve C. He argues the merits of A. Jane fights back with B. Dick offers C as a compromise, which was his intention all along. Dick wants Jane to agree to a vacation at a golf resort. He starts off with suggesting they go fishing. Jane declines. She suggests they go to a bed and breakfast in Amish country. Dick declines. Dick suggests a spa resort in Arizona. Jane agrees to the compromise. Dick had already planned to meet up with his buddies in Arizona, so it's a darn good thing Jane agreed. He doesn't tell her about that until they are on the plane, or they happen to meet his buddies at the hotel, which sets up a new conflict.

Call their bluff: Characters all make blanket statements and threaten things they'd never back up. Dick has a date with Jane for dinner. He needs to get out of it. He suggests Hooters. She reacts negatively and says she'd rather eat at a motorcycle dive bar. Since the motorcycle dive bar is exactly where Dick needs to meet his contact, he calls her bluff. Jane refuses to go with him, which suits Dick fine. The date is canceled. Dick needs to make a reservation at Jane's favorite five-star restaurant to make up for it. Jane may bravely state that she is willing to go to the dive bar against her better judgment to make a point. Dick agrees. Jane has a problem. She has to wriggle out of it or change her tactics. She can deflect or derail the conversation entirely.

Change the name: Changing the name of a thing can render it less objectionable and change the set of objections that accompany it. Dick asks Jane to steal something. She objects, naturally. He convinces her it isn't really stealing. It is borrowing or they are returning something to its rightful owner. Fanaticism is called religious freedom. This is rampant in terms of political correctness. Jane is likely to object to some things more than others. This also works if Jane refuses to grant Dick any ground. He switches tactics and gets her to disagree with his point's polar opposite.

Instead of arguing the merits of A, he argues the detriment of B. Therefore, if B is bad, A must be good. Dick might confuse her into agreeing with him.

☛ **Concede then deny**: Dick can listen to Jane rattle on and agree with her points, but refute her conclusion. This frustrates Jane into arguing her points all over again or stating them a different way so that Dick will accept her conclusion. He can either fight the conclusion, agree to disagree, or end or derail the conversation.

☛ **Cut it off**: If it is clear to Dick that he can't win, his best solution is to cut the conversation short or abruptly change the topic. Jane can use this tactic as a defense if Dick is attempting to bludgeon her into agreement.

☛ **Everyone does it**: This is a teenager's favorite ploy. They drag in people they've never met to support their side of the argument. Everyone is doing it, why can't I? It isn't really illegal if everyone is doing it. You've done it, why can't I? Aunt Sally did it. Uncle Ted says he did it all the time. These statements are either true or completely made up. They may be effective or fall flat depending on the audience.

☛ **Exaggerate it**: To effectively tear down Jane's argument, all Dick has to do is get her to exaggerate it. The simpler her logic is, the harder it is to refute. If Dick pushes her into generalizations, he has more ammunition to work with. He can compare apples to oranges. He can derail the conversation by arguing the generalities rather than the specifics.

Finish what he started: Dick wants Jane to do something, so he starts it then asks her to finish it for him. He can start a chore, a story, or a diversion tactic and ask Jane to finish it. It also works if Dick is in the middle of something. He asks Jane to do the other chore he wanted out of. He would take care of it if he could, but he's in the middle of something else. Would she be a dear and do it for him? This is a problem if the package he wants delivered contains cocaine.

Give then take: If Dick does something wonderful and unsolicited for Jane, she might feel she owes him one. She is more likely to accede to his next request, even if she is resistant. He can play the guilt card, "But I did X for you, why can't you do Y for me?"

Go for the kill: Jane has argued point after point. When she tries to change the subject or deflect the conversation, Dick knows he hit a weak spot. He may not know exactly what her weak spot is, but he was successful in his attempt. Dick has won. He can go in for the kill and drive the point home. He could give her some ground and restore equal footing. He can back away, satisfied that he met his objective. Either way, he made Jane rethink her position, question something she believed, or agree to something she resisted.

Jolly her into it: Dick makes a request. Jane declines. Dick teases her and pushes the boundaries of his request into the realm of stand-up comedy. He amplifies her objections to get her to laugh. She realizes her objections are kind of silly and agrees to his request.

Leave them laughing: If Dick needs to get out of an awkward or undesirable conversation, he can turn the situation into a one-man show. He can derail the situation by telling a joke or story to make everyone laugh and forget what they were discussing in the first place. If Jane is furious with Dick and he can make her laugh, she might forget why she was angry. If Jane wants something Dick doesn't want to deliver, he can make her laugh and forget her request.

Praise then please: Dick wants Jane to do something she hates. He butters her up first by telling her how much he loves her and appreciates her. He gets her feeling all warm and snuggly then pops the question. She would feel like a heel for refusing.

Question his authority: Jane may have an opinion, but may not be an authority on the subject. Dick may not be either, but all he has to do is instill reasonable doubt that she is accurate. He can state facts or invention to support his argument. Jane is forced to defend her authority rather than her idea. She doesn't have time to investigate his counterclaims or sources.

Shoot the messenger: Dick can publically discount everything Jane says simply because it is Jane saying it. He does not have to disprove what she is saying. All he has to do is cast sufficient doubt on her veracity. He can question her motives. He can insist that she is only saying what she says to further her own self-interest and it is not in the best interest of the situation. He can belittle her in front of other people.

☞ **The spider web**: Jane can draw Dick in slowly. Get him to agree to little things. Then hit him with her real request. If he has agreed that he likes popcorn and soda and time spent together, he will have a difficult time wriggling out of taking her to a chick flick.

☞ **Their words against them**: Dick can take something Jane says out of context and run with it. She wastes time trying to get him back to the original topic or becomes completely derailed and flustered while defending his detour. Dick can use a key word and catapult the conversation into another topic, perhaps the item he wanted to talk about all along.

☞ **Tick them off**: This is particularly effective as a counter measure. If Jane is grilling Dick about his alibi or strange behavior, he can start an argument about something else. He can insult her or goad her into losing her temper. Rationality flies out the window.

☞ **Timing is everything**: When persuading Jane, Dick must keep in mind the time, place, and her mindset. She is more willing to agree to something after a romantic weekend than after a fight. If he asks her over a candlelit dinner, she might be more receptive than she is while cleaning baby spit off her t-shirt.

☞ **Turn the table**: The best defense is a good offense. If Dick feels he is being targeted, he can turn the argument around on his opponent. He can latch onto inconsistencies and chip away at her logic. If Jane asks, "*Why do you think we're having this problem?*" He can answer, "*Why do you think we're having this problem?*" Answering a question with a question is a good deflection technique. This is especially useful if Dick is backed into a corner and cannot defend his choice or behavior with logic. He forces Jane to come up with viable justifications for him. He can also use Jane's arguments against her. Liars often use this tactic. The questioner often supplies a valid answer for them.

☞ **We're a team**: When asking Dick to do something he does not want to do, Jane emphasizes that they will be doing it *together.* She isn't asking him for a favor. She is asking him to spend time with her and help her achieve something. In fact, he will curry her favor by acquiescing and receive a reward for it. He is likely to give in.

☞ **Win-lose**: Rather than harp and complain, Jane can emphasize what Dick is missing out on if he doesn't comply. She explains how complying means he wins and not complying means he loses. This is time to sweeten the kitty, not bludgeon the other person into submission.

☞ **Win-win**: The best way to achieve success is to offer Dick a win-win scenario. The action benefits both Dick and Jane equally and no harm is done in the process. This method eliminates rational objections. It may overcome irrational objections.

Revision Tips

✍ Every conversation should offer some kind of tension. Key turning points require intense discussion. Highlight the areas where one character has to convince, or dissuade, another character.

✍ Which ploy did he use? There should be at least one.

✍ Does the tactic fit the situation? The scene objective may require more than one tactic. Dick may fail at one tactic and be forced to try a different tactic in a later scene.

✍ Did it work or not work?

✍ Is the character forced to try another tactic?

✍ Is the character forced to revisit the topic another time?

✍ Does he use the same tactic with different results or use a different tactic in a future scene?

BACKSTORY, DREAMS, & FLASHBACKS

Backstory, when used properly, enriches a plot. Used poorly, backstory creates a plot hole that your reader is forced to skip over or sludge through. Most readers skip past the boring bits.

The problem with backstory is often two-fold: too much too soon or way too much information. It is recommended that your novel not begin with backstory. Even when used as prologue, editors and agents frown upon it. You need to invest your readers in the current situation before trying to explain the character's history. Otherwise, they won't care.

Backstory can be related through dialogue, flashback, internal dialogue, thoughts, and narrative. Backstory can be presented in short bursts or can be presented as a scene with its own beginning, middle, and end. Be wary of information dumps. Backstory scenes should have tension and a scene goal.

Resist the urge to insert large sections of italicized words. You should be able to transition into and out of backstory without resorting to special fonts or italics.

The delicate balancing act is giving the reader enough backstory to help explain the current situation, but not so much that she is derailed from the forward momentum of the story. Backstory is not the same thing as a subplot set in the past when weaving separate story threads together.

Characters don't tell each other everything about themselves and their lives the first time they meet. If they do, their psychological boundaries are fuzzy. They make people nervous by offering too much information. You don't need to tell your readers everything up front either. If you do, your structure is fuzzy. Build a relationship with the reader first then begin sharing stories from the past.

Backstory works well in internal conflict scenes when your protagonist struggles with his personal dilemma. His personal dilemma can be rooted in his past. It could be the partner he didn't save, the girl he didn't get, or the friend he failed. The backstory makes the current situation more poignant and should be relevant to the overall story.

You can reveal your protagonist's critical flaw and secret weapon by explaining something that happened in the past. The critical flaw is revealed near the beginning to explain why Dick is drawn into the story problem and trips him up along the way. The flaw can have its roots in an episode from the past.

The secret weapon is revealed early on to explain why Dick, and only Dick, can solve the overall story problem. It can be a talent, strength of character, belief, or an actual object. You can show him using his secret weapon, or refusing to use it, in the past before he is called upon to use it in the present.

Whatever skills or failings Dick has, don't whip them out at the last minute by saying, "*Oh, yeah, back in school I used to* (fill in the blank)." That is backfilling and it's a no-no.

Backstory must, above all, be relevant. Don't spend paragraphs telling us about Dick's botany hobby unless he uses botany to solve the overall story problem. It bores your readers. They don't need to know about every Civil War battle, every lover the protagonist ever had, or the life stories of everyone who sank with the Titanic. Backstory that has no relationship to the current story is irritating. Readers flip past it or skim read it. If it happens often enough, they put the book down and walk away.

Backstory can raise questions rather than answer them. You can show Dick doing or saying something in the past, but not explain why. Mystery keeps the reader invested.

Backstory can be revealed in layers, like peeling an onion. Each reveal adds a slightly different twist to the reader's understanding of what happened.

Backstory can be used to create conflict. If Dick did something in the past, he can repeat the action or find himself in the same dilemma in the present timeframe, only there is an obstacle this time. His old method no longer works. He knows better now and this time it's uncomfortable.

Backstory can create conflict for Dick by presenting him with difficult choices. In the past, the decision might have been easy. The current situation, or new knowledge, makes the same choice more difficult.

Backstory can reveal change. If Dick is afraid of spiders because he was bitten by one as a child, he may have to take on the giant spiders that invaded Earth at the climax. If Dick was a coward in the past, he can be brave in the present. If Dick denied his feelings in the past, he can embrace them in the present.

Backstory can be revealed though dialogue. You must avoid the horrible "*As you know, Sally*" information dumps. Make sure your characters would utter the words in a real conversation.

Secrets, old wounds, a character's hot buttons, prejudices, and conceits can rear their ugly heads during heated conversations. It should be revealed through a verbal sparring match, not a lazy trot down memory lane. Dick should be trying to keep Jane from saying what needs to be said, revealing a painful secret, pointing out a person's flaws, or exposing old wounds.

Backstory in the form of letters or journal entries tests a reader's patience. They draw the reader out of real time. A few readers adore them. Most don't. I scan read them. If they are too long, I skip over them. They rarely contain conflict and are a lazy way of delivering information.

Writers often have a character write or read a letter or journal to impart historical information to the reader. There are instances where it works, but it is rarely done skillfully. These are sometimes placed in italics. If you insist on this device, keep it short and simple. Pages of italics strain the eyes.

If the contents can be summarized quickly through internal dialogue or dialogue, do that instead. We don't need to see a long news article about a body being found. Dick can read the article and comment on it to Sally, offering her the juicy parts. Most of us do this when we read something to someone across the kitchen table or office desk. We don't read the whole article. We react emotionally to the contents.

"I can't believe this garbage! Did you read this? It says ..."

"Listen to this, the Mayor thinks everyone should hang laundry outside to save on energy consumption. I don't want bird poop on my sheets."

We skip over the *blah, blah, blah* parts and read the good stuff.

"Referencing statistics on the dangers of cell phones, it says, yada, yada, yada, the police will start enforcing the texting ban on Friday. Better warn our kids."

This type of delivery keeps the reader in real time and in the presence of characters they care about.

Dreams are another potential plot hole. We all dream. Some people remember them; some don't. Dreams can be crazy, hallucinogenic thrill rides. If you use them in your fiction, they should be there for a reason. They should set up something or reveal something important to the character. Avoid the urge to relate dreams just because you had a really cool one and want to put it in there. As intriguing as your dream journal is to you, it won't be to your readers, particularly if it has nothing to do with the story. Dreams can feel contrived, so use them carefully and seldom. Transition in and out. They don't need to be italicized or offset.

Backstory can be told via prologue and epilogue, with the entire story told in flashback between the two "bookends." It irritates, rather than delights, if not done well. Many readers don't mind a prologue if it is intriguing. This rule is often broken to effect, particularly in Literary, Fantasy, and Thriller and Suspense genres.

In Thrillers, the story can begin with a scene from the antagonist's point of view. This is good if you are following a serial killer, not so good if you are listening to an angry spouse rant. It shouldn't attempt to tell the reader every little detail about your story world or the history of a situation before the action begins.

In Literary stories, we often first hear from the protagonist long after the events are over. The entire story is one long memoir with an epilogue that reinforces the wisdom gained.

In a Fantasy, the prologue sometimes sets up the time, place, and story world. If it is kept short, the reader might actually read it. Otherwise, they flip to Chapter 1. If necessary, they reference the prologue later. You should be able to fit in the crucial setup and history without using this device.

In a Suspense story, the prologue can set up the story problem in advance or hint at the ending before the beginning to set up suspense. You should be able to write suspense without this device, but it is certainly used.

Backstory can be related through narrative, but keep it short and simple. Transition in and out and don't offset it. A paragraph or two should suffice. A chapter or two of backstory loses the reader. She pages forward until she gets to the part that matters. That is not the kind of page turning to aim for.

It reminds me of a line from a movie uttered as a character ripped off the rear-view mirror in his car: "*What's behind me is not important.*" If the action has already passed, we know the characters lived to tell about it. It may have bearing on what is happening now, but the characters survived and have moved onto what is happening now. The reader may feel there is no need to worry about a long passage detailing what happened in the past if the characters are clearly functioning in the present.

Short snippets of backstory can be revealed through inner dialogue and thoughts. What a character thinks reveals character. A conversation or situation can bring back pleasant or unhappy memories. This is part of interiority.

Dick can think:

Sally thinks she knows everything. Even when we were in kindergarten, she thought she knew everything. No one in this town ever changes.

This reveals that he has a history with the town, he has known Sally since kindergarten, and he isn't too pleased with her. In this example, he keeps the negative opinion to himself. The same information could be related as dialogue. In the next example, Dick shares the same information and antagonizes Sally in the process.

"Yeah, you thought you knew everything back in kindergarten, too. Nothing ever changes in this town."

Jane might drive past her old house, the one she shared with her ex-husband, and think:

I missed the house. I loved the symmetry of it, the gables, and the white picket fence. I loved the rosebushes and the neighborhood cat that used to sun itself on the steps. A wave of hatred consumed me. Dick was such a lying, cheating, jerk. It was more than the divorce. It was losing my home. I should still be there, sitting on the front porch swing, drinking tea.

This reveals that Jane used to live in the house, her aesthetic preferences, her husband cheated on her, she likes tea, and she misses the house more than her ex. If Dick wants to win her back, he has a tough road ahead. It might help if he bribed the current owners into selling him the house. You could have spent pages telling us about Jane's past. Instead, it was summarized in a few short, bittersweet sentences.

Memories can be in the form of flashback. Keep them short and simple, a sentence or two. If a recollection is related as a full scene, it should contain action and dialogue, an obstacle and a solution. It should not be a narrative dump.

It helps to trigger memories with something the character sees, smells, touches, or tastes. It can be a person, place, or thing. Songs stick with us and can bring up a feeling or a forgotten person. Smells can take you back to a place and time and the person it reminds you of. Every time Dick sees the ocean on television, he may feel and smell saltwater in his nose. Every time Jane smells fresh baked cookies, it may remind her of the grandmother she adored. Every time Sally hears a train, it may remind her of her sad childhood. The neural connection is hard-wired. The response is involuntary.

A flashback is a transition in time. A character may have a quick flash of memory. It is expressed through his thoughts or interior dialogue. A flashback should reveal information or explain a specific character or event. It should relate to the current scene. Flashbacks can create speed bumps and should be used sparingly and only when the information cannot be slipped in another way.

If you must use a flashback, incorporate it into the action. Keep it short and resume real time as soon as possible. A few paragraphs work better than a few pages. Begin the flashback with a single-phrase transition, but avoid telling:

Dick remembered the last time he visited the ocean. He was with Sally and they were in love, until she left him.

A better transition would be:

Dick stared at the beach poster. The smell of saltwater filled his nose. He hated the ocean as much as he loved Sally, the scheming witch.

If Dick sees Sally again, the game is on. If she wants to woo him back, it would be wise to avoid the beach. If they meet on a beach, the conversation is likely to turn heated.

To format, you can switch from past tense to the past perfect tense for a sentence or two before reverting to the past tense again within the flashback.

End the flashback with another, short transition phrase to orient the reader to real time. You can use a trigger to bring them back to the present: a doorbell, a voice, a dog barking. Be subtle.

The train whistled. Dick flinched and turned away from the poster. Time to get back to work and lock Sally in the dark jail of the past where she belonged.

Revision Tips

✍ If your backstory flows organically, you shouldn't have to set it apart with special fonts or formatting. Read through your manuscript. Do you have large passages of italics or special formatting? Are they absolutely necessary? Can you change the flow so there is a smooth transition into and out of the backstory, flashback, memory, or dream?

✍ Do you use letters and journals? Can you cut them without sacrificing anything important? Are they taking up too much page time? Can the character summarize the contents? If you use them, do they contribute in a meaningful way? They should reveal something important, twist the story, or complicate the overall story problem. If they don't, cut them.

✍ Have you related dreams? Do they illuminate or complicate the story? If not, consider cutting them. Keep them short. Make them work for you instead of against you.

Diana Hurwitz

NARRATOR INTRUSION

The biggest problem with any point of view, other than omniscient, is narrator or narrative intrusion. Speaking to the audience was used in 18th and 19th century novels and in some modern Sit-Coms. The author interrupts the story to deliver his commentary, thoughts, opinions, or information, creating speed bumps that disrupt the reader's total immersion in the story. Comments, thoughts, opinions, and information should be filtered through the characters, not the writer.

Omniscient narrators are able to be in everyone's head at all times. They often intrude with their own opinion. You lose a certain number of readers with this method.

With other points of view, narrator intrusion removes the verbal camera from the shoulder or the eyes of the viewpoint character to take in action on the stage the character isn't aware of. The speed bumps can be low or high depending on the severity of the intrusion.

Intrusion is difficult to avoid. Stringent editing can fix it. Read each scene. If possible, have other people read each scene to look for intrusions. Pull back and look at what you've written with a jaundiced eye. Ask yourself if you've written anything the point of view character couldn't see, hear, feel, smell, taste, touch, notice, know, or do.

Key intrusion words to look for include: as before, after, behind, believed, considered, debated, discovered, during, felt, figured, hated, inside, knew, liked, loved, noticed, realized, pondered, remembered, sensed, since, smelled, tasted, thought, wanted to, when, while, wished, understood, until, used to.

When you've identified the intrusion, it is fairly easy to repair it. Rephrase it in a way the character would say it or do it. Writers are frequently cautioned to show not tell, though there are times when the character has to *tell*. It is a fine, hotly debated line and one most writers struggle with. Don't tell us someone is sad, show us. Don't tell us someone is angry, show us. The advice makes many writers throw darts at their manuscript.

Showing versus telling is not necessarily the same as narrator intrusion. An example of intrusion would be:

Sam Malone, a dark, handsome, intelligent man stared through the window of his fortieth floor penthouse at the brooding LA skyline.

This sentence is simply awful, but you get the point. Yes, I just intruded with an opinion. If you are writing in omniscient, this is perfectly acceptable. In all other cases, it isn't. Even in third person, a character does not think to himself:

I'm a handsome, intelligent, man standing in my fortieth floor penthouse. My décor is ultra modern and shows I have expensive taste.

To fix the intrusion, the writer can show the character entering his building or getting off at the fortieth floor. The character places his keys in a ceramic bowl on a glass and steel hall table or hangs them on an ornate message board above it. The character walks into the living room, across the deep pile carpet, and places his jacket on the back of a white leather sofa. He can look at himself in the mirror (overused but effective) or catch a glimpse of himself in the glass as he stares at the brooding LA skyline.

He could notice a photo of himself and his wife. He can think about the way they used to be, so young, so good looking, so idealistic. He can wonder if she still finds him as attractive as he finds her. He can miss her presence in his swank apartment, one they chose together but he now occupies alone. In this way, you show the reader his world rather than tell them about it.

Another example is where the writer inserts statements for suspense:

Sally didn't know that Dick had other plans for her and that his plans would change her life forever.

Little did Dick know that Spot, so peacefully curled up at the end of his bed, would attack him in the middle of the night. If he had known what the dog was capable of, he might have put Spot in his crate.

These are extreme examples, but you get the point. Who is giving us this information? It isn't Dick or Sally. Some writers do this on purpose, to say, *"Wait for it … a tense situation is coming."* It does the opposite. The author just told us there is going to be an attack in the middle of the night, removing the suspense factor.

The author could have shown Dick snuggling up with dear Spot, holding the dog close, feeling all warm and safe. Then Spot growls and wriggles away from Dick. The dog's fur stands on end. Cut scene. Next chapter. The reader keeps reading to find out what upset the dog. That is well-crafted suspense.

In third person limited point of view and first person, a writer often tells the reader things the point of view character couldn't possible know.

Jane sat in the café, sipping a cooling mocha latte, lost in thought, a book open on the table. The man in the booth behind her stared and wondered why someone so good looking was so sad.

Unless Jane has eyes in the back of her head, she isn't aware that she is being watched. Unless she reads minds, she won't know what the man behind her is thinking. The verbal camera panned away from Jane and followed the man in the booth. This is either head-hopping or author intrusion, depending on the point of view. Another example would be:

Sally perched on the edge of a park bench. She closed her eyes, wiping the sweat from her brow. When did it get so hot? A man sat down on the grass, not close enough to be obvious, but near enough to catch her if she decided to run.

Sounds suspenseful, right? However, Sally's eyes are closed. She can't see the man sitting on the grass. She doesn't know why he is sitting on the grass, or that he intends to grab her if she leaves the bench. The author thinks he is setting up suspense, but he is shifting point of view or intruding. The scene can be fixed by simply having Sally open her eyes, see the guy sitting on the grass. She can decide he is a problem and calculate whether she could run before he could grab her. This keeps us in her head and sets the tension. Will she go for it? Will she make it?

Writing in first person POV, a passage might read:

I bent over to pick up the note that fell from the boy's backpack. The paper was crumpled, from the kind of yellow legal pad a businessman would use. I unfolded it and examined the

147

crabbed handwriting. A red stain colored my cheeks as the profane words registered. What kind of boy would write such a thing?

This is very subtle intrusion. Why? Because the character can't see her own face, so how would she know it was red? She could feel her face flush. The reader knows that a flushed face looks red. You don't have to explain it. These mistakes are hard to catch. A good critique partner, beta-reader, or editor helps you find them.

Another example is when the author gives the reader the reason for someone else's behavior:

Jane lifted the hotel receipt from the table. She held it up so Dick could get a good look at it. "And you were at the Savoy last week for what reason?" Dick turned away to hide his panic and formulate an excuse.

If the piece is written in omniscient point of view, this passage works. Otherwise, it doesn't. Jane can see Dick turn away. She might guess why, but she wouldn't think to herself:

Dick turned away to hide his panic and formulate an excuse.

Jane could see him turn away. She can surmise that he is hiding something and press Dick for an answer. Dick's lack of response tells her he is formulating a lie. When he comes out with, "*It was a business meeting,*" Jane assumes it is a lie.

Jane can then call him on it by saying something like:

"An overnight meeting?"

Dick justifies it with:

"No, but it ran late and I was tired, so I got a room."

Jane could top it off with:

"You paid for a room instead of a cab? We only live five blocks away."

Lie exposed and you have tense dialogue with a great zinger at the end. The fight is on.

Another problem is describing details a character would never notice.

Dick is standing at the coffee machine in the break room and Jane walks in with designer shoes and a dress that hugs her curves. Unless he is really into fashion or works in the fashion industry, he won't know the dress is Dior and the shoes are Manolo Blahnik. A lot of female readers won't know what the heck Dior or Manolos look like either. It is best to describe the dress and the response it creates within Dick (he is turned on by stiletto heels), than to toss in labels a man (or woman) wouldn't recognize.

The author might know all about fashion or might throw designer names in to impress or to define character. It can have the opposite effect if the reader is frustrated by not grasping the reference. When a writer inserts cultural, geographical, designer, celebrity, and product references, she assumes her readers are familiar with them. When the references are lost on the reader, he flips the page. He might waste time Googling the reference. In order to Google, he must put the book down or switch screens. This is not the kind of page turning to aim for.

A reader forgives a few of these. If the book is riddled with them, and he feels the need to Google, you may lose him forever to Facebook and Twitter.

You can use the shorthand references for inspiration, but you need to describe it. You can say:

Jane had on a tight, knee-length dress and uncomfortable-looking heels.

This statement reveals character more than blatant references. If a man observing a woman thinks her dress is too tight and her shoes interfere with her ability to walk, it tells you he is either sizing her up as a potential victim who can't outrun him, or deciding that she would make a very high-maintenance girlfriend. He might like women who dress like runway models or prefer a girl who wears cargo shorts and sneakers. The way he describes Jane's outfit tells us a lot about the way he views women.

Revision Tips

✍ Read through your manuscript. Have you intruded with thoughts, opinions, or descriptions from non-viewpoint characters? If so, fix them.

✍ Are the descriptions limited to what the character can see, hear, smell, taste, touch, and know about?

✍ Have you planted false suspense? Can you change it?

✍ Can you spot the places where you, the author, are intruding with your thoughts, opinions, and observations? Cut them or revise them to reflect the character's lens.

✍ Have you used cultural references as shorthand instead of describing them?

LEVEL TWO: WORD CHOICE

Grammar is the ringmaster that whips clauses, phrases, and words into recognizable formations. It encompasses spelling and punctuation. It governs word usage, parts of speech, sentence and paragraph structure, and punctuation. It is said that English is one of the hardest languages to learn. It has more exceptions than rules and defies logic some of the time.

This section is not meant to be a textbook on grammar. Those are fairly thick tomes. It is meant to be a reference during revision passes. If English isn't your native language, don't rely on this section to teach it to you. I'm sure I've left something critical out. If you speak a foreign language, it won't help you either. My knowledge is limited to French and German 101 taken in high school thirty years ago and a few swear words I picked up along the way.

What separates a master writer from a rookie is often his use of the English language. In the right hands, words flow from sentence to sentence, paragraph to paragraph, and page to page in a silken stream. It immerses your reader in your story world and keeps them there until you are ready to let them go.

The problems begin when a writer either mangles the language or tries to use words too cleverly. When word choice calls attention to itself, it becomes a distraction from the story.

The purpose of this revision layer is to consider your word choices and sentence structure carefully, to suggest that you progress ideas rather than repeat yourself, and to help you write with intention.

We cover basic precepts and utilize them to polish your prose.

NOUNS AND PRONOUNS

A noun identifies who, where, and what. It is a person, place, or thing. It can be a subject, subject complement, indirect object, object, or object of a preposition.

If you remember diagramming sentences in high school, you should be able to reduce every sentence to a subject and verb. Subjects can be objects, nouns, or pronouns. Subjects can be modified with adjectives, phrases, modifiers, and clauses.

☒ **The subject** is the thing performing the action of the verb.

<u>Dog</u> runs.

<u>Bird</u> flies.

<u>Man</u> thinks.

☒ **The subject complement** is the thing the noun is being linked to.

The dog (subject) is (verb) a <u>mongrel</u> (complement).

Dick (subject) is (verb) a <u>man</u> (complement).

☒ **The direct object** is the thing the verb is performing the action on.

The dog (subject) ate (verb) the <u>snack</u> (object).

The cat (subject) chased (verb) the <u>mouse</u> (object).

☒ **The indirect object** precedes the direct object and tells to us who the verb is being done for and tells us who receives a direct object. Indirect objects require an object. They are used with verbs such as: *bring, give, offer, show, take,* and *tell.*

Dick (subject) offered (verb) <u>me</u> (indirect object) a car (direct object).

Sally (subject) took (verb) the ball (direct object) from <u>Jane</u> (indirect object).

☒ **The object of a preposition** is a noun or pronoun that follows a preposition (*after, as, at, before, by, for, from, like, of, on, out of, through, to, toward*) and completes its meaning.

Dick drove to (preposition) the <u>supermarket</u> (object).

Sally walked through (preposition) the <u>mall</u> (object).

☒ A phrase consisting of a preposition, its object, and any of the object's modifiers is called a **prepositional phrase**.

These are basic noun rules. The important part when revising is to make certain all nouns fulfill their intended function and are not part of run-on or incomplete sentences.

☒ Abstract versus Concrete Nouns

Concrete nouns are items you can see, hear, smell, taste, or feel. Abstract nouns are items such as ideas or concepts and often end in *ity* or *ness*.

Duplicate versus duplicity.

Hate versus hatefulness.

☒ Modifying Nouns

In terms of revision, nouns can be modified by adjectives and modifying phrases. A modifying phrase could be a cliché. A strong noun is considered better than a noun with an adjective tacked on. See the sections on adjectives and clichés.

Sally (subject), whom we all love (modifying phrase), will be there.

Delightful (adjective) Jane (subject) will be there too.

157

☒ Common Nouns

Common nouns refer to nonspecific people, places, and things. Common nouns are not usually capitalized. When it comes to plural nouns, see the rules relating to collective nouns.

☒ Proper Nouns

Proper nouns are the formal names for people, places, and things. It includes first, middle, and surnames, cities, companies, countries, monuments, states, and works of art. They should always be capitalized. Make sure they are used and spelled correctly.

One thing to watch out for is using people names in dialogue. There are very few instances when we refer to someone we are talking to by name. We say his name to get his attention. We say it to caution him. We say it when we introduce him. We only use his middle name if we are really angry. Otherwise, we often revert to endearments or nicknames. This is the arena for the *"you know, Sally"* information dump. If you have Dick refer to Sally by name when he is talking to her, it should only happen once or twice for emphasis. It should not be used to avoid dialogue tags. It may be necessary on occasion. That occasion should not be every other line of dialogue.

Acceptable: "Jack mentioned you weren't at the office on Monday," Dick said.

Unacceptable: "As you know, Jack, I didn't see you at the office on Monday," Dick said.

☒ Pronouns

Pronouns are a little complicated. Pronouns have a case and shift in their form with the case. Within a sentence, pronouns may function as a subject, direct object, object of preposition, or indirect object. The important thing when searching for these words is to make sure they are used correctly.

Demonstrative pronouns identify a noun or a pronoun: *that, this, these,* and *those.*

This and *that* are singular.

These and *those* are plural.

That is also a relative pronoun.

This and *these* refer to things that are close in terms of space or time.

That and *those* refer to things that are far away in terms of space or time.

Indefinite pronouns refer to an unspecified person, place or thing and suggest all, any, none, or some: *all, another, any, anybody, anyone, anything, each, every, everybody, everyone, everything, few, many, nobody, none, one, several, some, somebody,* and *someone.* Indefinite pronouns can also be used as adjectives.

We invited everyone but nobody came.

We are the few, serving the many, to benefit no one.

Interrogative pronouns pose questions: *what, whatever, which, whichever, who, whoever, whom,* and *whoever.*

Who and *whom* refer to people.

Who is the subject of a verb.

Whom is the object of a verb.

Which and *what* refer to things and animals.

Which and *what* can also be used as adjectives.

Intensive pronouns emphasize their antecedents and are the same as reflexive pronouns: *herself, himself, itself, myself, ourselves, themselves, yourself,* and *yourselves.*

I myself would never go there.

He said it himself, he is his own worst enemy.

Objective personal pronouns serve as the object of a verb, compound verb, preposition, or infinitive phrase: *her, him, it, me, them, us,* and *you.*

Tell him I love her.

If left up to me, I'd never pick him.

It was never the same afterward.

Possessive pronouns define ownership: *hers, his, its, mine, ours, theirs,* and *yours.*

What makes you think it is yours?

It's not mine, it's his.

It's not yours, it's ours.

Reflexive pronouns refer to the subject of the clause of the sentence: *herself, himself, itself, myself, ourselves, themselves, yourself,* and *yourselves.*

Suit yourselves, I'll drive myself to Chicago.

Relative pronouns link one phrase or clause to another phrase or clause: *which, whichever, who, whoever, whom,* and *whomever.*

Whichever way you decide, I'll support you.

Whoever said it, they were wrong.

Subjective personal pronouns replace a proper noun and act as the subject of the sentence: *he, I, it, she, they, we,* and *you.*

I scream. You scream. We all scream for ice cream.

Between you and me, they are all crazy.

☒ Collective Nouns

A collective noun indicates a group of people or things. You must determine whether a collective noun is singular or plural and which verb tense to use with it. The secret is deciding if the collective noun is performing the act as one unit or performing the act as separate units.

If they are all doing the same thing at the same time, they are singular.

The team (it) raced onto the field to begin the game.

The corporation (it) sold off its shares.

If they are not all doing the same thing at the same time, they are plural. They can behave in a similar fashion, but act as individuals.

The team (they) returned to the gym to shower and change clothes.

The corps (they) dispersed to their home bases.

If you are unsure, insert the word *members* after the collective noun (*team members, jury members*) to make it plural. The second option is to change the word entirely and use a different noun such as *students* instead of *team*, and *soldiers* instead of *corps*.

A dozen eggs should do it.

Dozens came over on the Mayflower.

A band is coming for dinner.

The jury has reached a verdict.

The senate entered and took their seats.

Collective nouns can be made plural: *families, groups,* and *teams.*

A list of collective nouns to search for:

army	collective	family	lot
assembly	colony	firm	mass
audience	committee	fleet	mess
band	company	flight	minority
batch	congregation	flock	mob
battery	constellation	gaggle	muster
bevy	convention	galaxy	navy
board	cornucopia	gang	nest
brigade	cortege	gross	number
bundle	corps	group	orchestra
business	council	handful	pack
cabinet	crew	heap	pantheon
camp	crowd	herd	parliament
caravan	deck (cards)	hive	phalanx
cast	department	host	plague
cavalcade	division	house	platoon
chorus	dozen	huddle	pod
circus	drove	judiciary	posse
class	ensemble	jury	pride (lions)
clique	faculty	kind	public

quiver	salon	squad	tabernacle
rabble	school	stable	tribe
range	sea	staff	troupe
regatta	senate	stash	yoke
round (drinks)	slew	swarm	
run	society	team	

Companies, organizations, teams, bands, orchestras, and musical groups take on a singular form even when they are plurals.

The ensemble was magnificent last night.

General Motors is closing five plants.

Starbucks is building another store.

Puccini's serves excellent food.

Even if the word a*ssociates* is tacked onto the end, it is still a single entity.

Smith, Jones, and Associates is on the side of the defense. (spellcheck will tell you this is wrong. You can fix it by stating "the firm of" or ignoring spellcheck).

The firm of Alias, Smith, and Jones is defending the perpetrator.

Proctor and Gamble is moving its headquarters to Japan.

Sport teams are the opposite. They are considered plural regardless of whether the words are plural.

The Colts are not winning this year.

The Reds play the Red Sox next week.

When the team is referred to by the city in which it resides, use the singular verb.

Cincinnati needs to sign a good pitcher this year.

Revision Tips

✍ Do a search, [Control] [F] or Find. for pronouns and noun phrases.

✍ Are you using them correctly?

✍ Are they unnecessarily repetitive?

✍ When it comes to pronouns, is the noun they reference clear? If you have multiple instances of the same pronoun in a sentence or paragraph, make sure they need to be there and that they make sense.

✍ Are all proper nouns spelled correctly and consistently?

✍ Have you used a person's name in dialogue? If so, should you cut it?

ADJECTIVES

"When you catch an adjective, kill it." ~ Mark Twain.

Adjectives modify nouns or pronouns and should be located by or near the noun. When performing the adjective revision pass you can do a search and kill for each word in your manuscript (faster) or read through your printed manuscript and highlight or underline them (slower).

Take a hard look at each and every one. The point is not to kill all adjectives. It is to use them judiciously for impact rather than using them out of laziness. If you use the same adjectives over and over, keep one or two instances. Find other descriptive words to replace the rest. It's like working out at a gym; the more often you do it, the stronger you become.

The general consensus is that many adjectives are overused and add little definition to a sentence. Adjectives often indicate telling instead of showing. Weak adjectives don't tell enough. They don't explain why something is pretty or ugly. Unnecessary adjectives have already been implied or are redundant, such as white snow (see the section on redundancies). Too many adjectives in a row diminish each other. The same adjective repeated more than once in a paragraph is overkill.

The point critics make is that it is better to explain why the character thinks something is ugly or describe what they feel is ugly than write: *He was ugly*. Ugly to one person could be beautiful to another. You could dress up the adjective by repeating it in an effective cumulative sentence:

Dick grinned. It made him ugly, the kind of ugly that emanates from the core, that furrows the face, thins the lips, and narrows the eyes, the kind of ugly even a mother couldn't bear to look at.

In this instance, you are repeating the word *ugly* intentionally and skillfully. It would be a terrific way to describe an antagonist as he enters the story. It would be over the top to describe a secondary character that way. Cumulative sentences are used for maximum impact and should be used sparingly.

Adjectives sprinkled here and there keep prose from sounding too clinical. Use them like salt: a little goes a long way and don't pour them all into the same sentence.

Sometimes you have to compare two objects or describe the way a character views something.

Adjectives take the form of positives, comparatives, and superlatives, such as *big, bigger,* and *biggest.*

A few have irregular forms:

bad, worse, worst

good, better, best

little, less, least

much, many

some, more, most

far, further, furthest

Proper adjectives are derived from proper nouns and refer to nationality, religious affiliation, or culture. The first letter is capitalized: *American, Arab, African, Asian, Australian, Caucasian, Catholic, French, German, Hindu, Italian, Jewish, Latino, Lutheran, Pakistani, Mexican,* and *Spanish.*

A few common adjectives include:

Appearance

adorable	bleary	chubby	crumpled
animated	blond	clean	curly
arrogant	bold	cluttered	cute
attractive	bony	colorful	dappled
auburn	bright	colorless	dazzling
awkward	brilliant	corkscrew	dismal
beautiful	brunette	crinkled	distinctive
becoming	calm	crisp	distinguished

drab
dramatic
drawn
dusky
ebony
elegant
energetic
exhausted
exotic
expensive
exuberant
fair
fancy
fearful
feminine
fey
fiery
flamboyant
flashy
flowery
flushed
formal
fragile
frail
freckled
fresh
frightened
frilled
frizzy
gamin
gaudy
gaunt
gigantic
glamorous

glassy
glimmering
glistening
gloomy
glossy
glowing
good-looking
gorgeous
grimy
handsome
healthy
homely
hysterical
immense
imposing
indistinct
lacy
lavish
lethargic
lifeless
lively
locks
long
magnificent
manly
massive
messy
morose
muscular
nappy
nervous
old-fashioned
opulent
pale

passive
pasty
peaceful
pensive
pimply
plain
pleasant
portly
pot-bellied
pretty
radiant
ragged
rigid
robust
rosy
rotund
rough
ruffled
rugged
quaint
queer
quiet
satiny
shabby
showy
shiny
short
shy
silky
slender
somber
sparkling
spiral
stately

stolid
stony
stout
studious
supple
tan
tantalizing
tearful
terrified
thin
tidy
timid
tiny
toothless
tranquil
tumescent
ugly
unattractive
ungainly
unsightly
vivacious
vivid
voluptuous
voluminous
wacky
weepy
whiny
wide-eyed
wild-eyed
wiry
wistful
woeful

Colors

amber
amethyst
aqua
aquamarine
aubergine
avocado
beige
black
blue
brass
brindle
bronze
brown
buff
burgundy
burnt umber
canary
carmine
carnelian
charcoal
chartreuse
citrine
claret
cerise
cherry
chestnut

chocolate
chrome
clear
cobalt
copper
coral
cordovan
cream
crimson
cyan
ebony
ecru
emerald
fuchsia
garnet
gold
gray
green
henna
indigo
iron
ivory
jade
jet
khaki
lavender

lemon
lilac
lime
magenta
maroon
mauve
mahogany
maize
mint
mustard
navy
obsidian
ochre
olive
onyx
orange
orchid
peach
pearl
pink
platinum
plum
poppy
primrose
puce
purple

red
rose
ruby
rust
saffron
sable
salmon
sapphire
scarlet
sepia
sienna
silver
slat
spruce
tan
topaz
turquoise
ultramarine
umber
vermilion
violet
walnut
white
wine
yellow

Condition

alive	famous	mushy	uninterested
better	fretful	odd	vast
careful	gifted	powerful	wrong
clever	helpful	rich	
dead	important	shy	
easy	inexpensive	tender	

Feelings (negative)

ambivalent	entitled	indolent	repulsive
angry	exhausted	irate	sad
anxious	fearful	irritated	scary
arrogant	fierce	jealous	snobbish
bewildered	fretful	lazy	thoughtless
boastful	garrulous	lonely	triumphant
clumsy	grumpy	mysterious	uptight
concerned	hateful	needy	urgent
contemptuous	helpless	nervous	wired
defeated	hurtful	obnoxious	worried
disgusted	hysterical	panicky	
distasteful	itchy	pessimistic	
embarrassed	indifferent	proud	

Feelings (positive)

accepting	calm	grateful	proud
affectionate	delightful	glowing	relieved
agreeable	eager	happy	silly
amiable	exuberant	jolly	thankful
bashful	exultant	joyful	upbeat
benevolent	faithful	kind	victorious
boastful	friendly	lively	witty
bounteous	gentle	nice	zealous
bountiful	gleeful	obedient	
brave	gracious	optimistic	

Quantity

abundant	full	numerous	substantial
bushel	heavy	peck	
empty	light	spare	
few	many	sparse	

Shape

aquiline	crooked	high	rectangular
angle	cube	hollow	round
arc	curved	horizontal	serpentine
arched	cylinder	low	shallow
ball	cylindrical	narrow	skinny
box	deep	octagon	spiral
broad	diagonal	orb	square
chubby	disc	oval	sphere
circle	discoid	ovate	steep
circular	ellipse	pentagon	straight
concave	elliptical	pentagonal	tetrahedral
cone	fanned	plane	trapezoid
conical	flat	polyhedron	triangle
concentric	helix	pyramid	triangular
convex	hexagon	pyramidal	wide
corkscrew	hexagonal	rectangle	

Sight

adjacent	branded	clean	crystalline
animated	breadth	clear	cupped
arid	bright	cluttered	curled
arrogant	brilliant	congested	curly
awkward	bruised	contoured	dappled
baggy	calm	crested	dark
blazing	charred	crisp	dazzling
blotched	checkered	crowded	decorative
bold	cheap	crowned	deep

depressed
depth
dingy
dirty
dismal
dotted
drab
dramatic
drooping
dull
dun
elegant
energetic
erect
exhausted
exotic
fat
fiery
filthy
flashy
fleshy
flowery
fluid
flushed
formal
fragile
frail
freckled
fresh
gigantic
girth
glassy
glazed
globe
glossy
glowing
grimy
grizzled
handsome

hardy
healthy
heavy
hemisphere
high
huge
immense
imposing
irresistible
iridescent
jammed
jeweled
lanky
large
lavish
lean
length
light
lithe
lively
long
loose
massive
messy
milky
miniature
mottled
muddy
muscular
narrow
nervous
new
old
opalescent
opaque
opulent
orderly
overloaded
packed

pale
palmate
parallel
patina
patterned
perky
pied
pinnate
plate
pleasant
plump
pretty
pristine
protruding
radiant
ramshackle
regal
reticulated
rigid
robust
rolling
rotted
ruddy
scrubbed
sinuous
serene
shabby
shallow
sharp
sheer
shimmering
shiny
short
showy
shy
sickly
slender
slim
small

smoky
snowy
solid
sooty
sparkling
spiked
spotted
square
stout
stately
straight
streamlined
stretched
striped
strong
sturdy
sunken
supple
swollen
tall
tantalizing
terrain
thick
thin
thread
tidy
tied
tight
timid
tiny
tired
translucent
transparent
triangle
twinkling
ugly
unsettled
untidy
upset

used wide wormlike young.
veined width worn
vertical wild wrinkled

Size:

big huge miniature strength
circumference immense miniscule tall
colossal large microscopic teeny
degree length petite teensy
dimension little proportioned tiny
extent magnitude puny towering
fat mammoth scaled wide
gigantic massive scrawny
great measurement short
height midget small

Smell

acidic flowery nauseating sharp
acrid fragrant odiferous sickly
aromatic fresh odor skunky
balmy gamy perfumed smoky
biting gaseous piney sour
briny heady plastic spicy
burned lemony pungent spoiled
citrus lilac putrid stagnant
cloying lime rancid stench
damp loamy redolent stinking
dank malodorous reeking suffocating
dirty mildewed rosy sweaty
doggy minty rotten sweet
earthy moist savory tart
fetid moldy scented tempting
fishy musty scorched

Time

ancient	late	quick	swift
brief	long	rapid	young
early	modern	short	
delayed	old	slow	
fast	old-fashioned	soon	

Taste

acidic	crunchy	oily	sweet
alkaline	curdled	overripe	tangy
bitter	delicious	peppery	tart
bittersweet	fishy	ripe	tasteless
bold	fruity	raw	tepid
briny	gingery	rotten	unripe
burned	hot	salty	vinegary
buttery	icy	sour	watery
cold	medicinal	spicy	weak
creamy	melted	spoiled	yummy
crisp	nutritious	stringy	

Touch

abrasive	clammy	cushioned	filthy
beaded	coarse	damaged	fine
biting	cold	damp	flaky
boiling	cool	dank	fleshy
breezy	corded	dirty	fluffy
broken	corrugated	downy	fluted
bubbled	cottony	dry	foamy
bubbly	creamy	dusty	fragile
bumpy	creepy	elastic	freezing
burning	crooked	embossed	furry
bushy	crisp	engraved	fuzzy
chapped	cuddly	feathery	glossy
chilly	curly	fiery	greasy

grimy	nappy	scalding	spiky
gripped	nubby	scaled	splintered
gritty	numb	scaly	steamy
grooved	numbing	scarred	sticky
hairy	oily	scorching	stinging
hard	pierced	scratchy	strong
heavy	pocked	sculptured	stubby
hot	polished	searing	tangled
icy	pressed	shaggy	tender
inlaid	prickly	sharp	tepid
itchy	pulpy	sheen	thick
keen	ragged	sheer	thin
kiss	raspy	shiny	tickling
knobby	raw	silky	tough
lacey	ridged	slick	tweedy
leathery	rocking	slimy	uneven
loose	rocky	slippery	warm
lukewarm	rough	smooth	waxy
matte	rubbery	soapy	weak
metallic	rutted	soft	wet
moist	sandy	sopping	woolly
mushy	satiny	spongy	velvety

Revision Tips

✍ Do a search on the above list (and your favorites) and check for repetitive usage. The same word one or two times throughout the manuscript is fine. Every other paragraph is not. To do a search hit [Control] [F] and Highlight All or Find Next. Save frequently using [Control] [S]. You can also highlight or underline adjectives in your printed manuscript.

✍ Read through the draft. If you used an adjective in a sentence, is it needed? Does it add something worthwhile? If not, consider cutting it or replacing it with a more effective description.

✍ Are your nouns doing their job without the adjectives? If not, can you choose stronger nouns?

ADJECTIVAL CLAUSES

An adjectival or relative clause modifies a noun, noun phrase, or pronoun. If the clause does not meet these criteria, it may be a comma splice.

✐ A relative clause must contain a subject and a verb.

✐ It must begin with a relative pronoun (*that, which, who, whom, whose*) or a relative adverb (*when, where, wherein, why*).

✐ It must answer a question: *how many, what kind,* or *which one*.

✐ The subject and verb follows the relative pronoun or adverb.

✐ The relative pronoun serves as the subject and has a verb.

A relative clause cannot stand alone or it becomes a sentence fragment. To recognize this error, read the sentence. A relative clause should follow the word it describes.

Dick offered (subject/verb) a hug (object), <u>which</u> (pronoun) Jane (subject) declined (verb).

The relative phrase modified the word *hug.*

I said (subject/verb) goodnight (object) to my husband (modifier), <u>who</u> (subject) continued to watch (modified verb) sports (object) with his eyes closed (modifies watch).

The relative phrase modified the word *husband.*

A relative clause must be punctuated correctly. For each clause, you have to decide if it is essential or nonessential. If it is essential (the phrase cannot be removed without changing the meaning), you do not need a comma.

The students who were lounging in the hall were asked to take their seats.

It is important to keep the "were lounging in the halls" part. This sentence could be further tightened.

The students lounging in the hall were asked to take their seats.

If the clause is nonessential, use a comma.

Dick and Jane, who dine out often, were excited about going to the steakhouse.

You could remove the phrase. How often they dine out doesn't change the fact that they were going to dine out.

The effective use of relative clauses is covered in the section on sentence structure.

Watch out for too many clauses that begin with *what, which,* and *who.* They are used to support a noun. See if you can find a more effective noun or replace the phrase with a single descriptive word. If not, use these phrases sparingly.

Who is nominative, *whose* is possessive, and *whom* is objective.

If you can substitute *I, he,* or *she,* use *who.*

If you can substitute *him, her, they,* or *them,* use *whom.*

If you are referring to ownership, use *whose. Who's* is a contraction for *who is.*

Clauses that begin with *who* are independent of the rest of the sentence. It is important to identify the object it modifies in the sentence. The subject in the sentence is not necessarily the object of modification.

<u>I</u> am the one <u>who</u> failed you.

<u>She</u> is the one <u>who</u> hates you.

I am the one <u>whom</u> <u>they</u> blame. (whom refers to they, not I).

The sentence works without *whom.*

I am the one they blame.

It is Ted whom they flock to.

Whom refers to *they*, not Ted.

This sentence also works without *whom*.

It is Ted they flock to.

Who do they blame?

Who refers to the unnamed subject not *they*.

Revision Tips

✍ Make sure your noun and clause work together. Avoid comma splices. If the clause is nonessential, make sure you inserted commas. If the clause is essential, remove commas.

✍ Do a search for relative pronouns (*that, which, who, whom, whose*). Make sure they are used correctly.

✍ Do a search for relative adverbs (*when, where, wherein, why*). Make sure they are used correctly.

MODIFYING PHRASES

Modifying phrases can begin with a participle (*verb* + *ing*), adverb, pronoun, or a phrase that backtracks and picks up a word from the base clause. It does not contain both a subject and verb and cannot stand alone.

✏ **Participle phrases** modify nouns and pronouns. The present participle of a verb refers to ongoing actions and ends in *ing*. The past participle of a verb refers to a completed or past action and ends in *e, ed, en, t* or *n*.

Dick slept, <u>sprawling</u> across the king-sized bed.

Jane slept, <u>curled</u> up in her favorite blanket.

✏ **Noun modifiers** usually precede the noun like adjectives. They can, and sometimes must, follow it.

The <u>sleeping</u> children snored softly.

The children snored softly, <u>sleeping</u> on top of one another like puppies.

✎ **Gerund phrases** contain a verb that has been turned into a noun by adding *ing*.

Used as a subject: <u>Hiking</u> is hard work.

Used as a direct object: Dick went <u>hiking</u>.

Used as a subject complement: Dick's favorite activity is <u>hiking</u>.

Used as the object of a preposition: Dick missed work to go <u>hiking</u>.

Used as an appositive (substitute for previous noun or pronoun): <u>Hiking</u> having become an addiction, Dick spent all of his free time in the woods.

✎ Infinitive phrases (using *to* plus verb form) can act as nouns, adjectives, or adverbs.

<u>To kick</u> the ball, Dick had to cross the field.

<u>To remain</u> employed, Dick must have perfect attendance.

✎Prepositional phrases begin with prepositions.

after	by	near	under
as	for	of	until
at	from	on	up
because of	in	over	with
before	in front of	through	
behind	in regard to	to	
between	like	together with	

Dick completed the hike <u>after</u> he left work.

Dick kicked the ball <u>as</u> he crossed the field.

Dick quit work <u>with</u> no notice.

Phrases beginning with *as* indicate that two things are being done simultaneously. In the above example, Dick kicks the ball as he crosses the field. He can't physically do so. He must pause for a second to kick the ball then cross the field. The action combines two separate propositions. It is generally considered that all *as* adverb phrases should be cut. If you keep them, make sure the acts can physically be done at the same time and that the phrase is necessary.

✎ Modifying phrases are formed in a number of ways.

Begin with a verb phrase:

Jane ran away, screaming for help.

Sally sat, blinded by her tears.

Dick sobbed, driven to despair.

Begin with a verb plus another modifier such as an adverb:

Jan turned away, grinning widely.

Sally ignored her, momentarily distracted by the waiter.

Begin with an article plus the subject or object from the base clause:

Jane opened the book, a book she was forbidden to touch.

A woman opened the book, a brave, mad woman.

Begin with an article plus an adjective plus the noun from the base clause:

Jane opened the book, an ancient book.

The book lay on the table, a dangerous book.

Begin with an article plus an adjective plus almost any noun followed by a prepositional phrase:

Jane closed the book, a smile lighting her face.

Jane closed the book, the words filling her with unease.

Jane closed the book, her ribbon marking the page.

Begin with an article plus an appositive or noun phrase for one of the base clause nouns:

Jane closed the book, an emboldened woman prepared to fight the ghost.

Jane closed the book, the answer to all of her questions.

Jane closed the book, the repository of secret lore.

Begin with a possessive pronoun referring to the subject, object, or sense of the base clause:

Jane closed the book, its fragile pages crackling.

Jane closed the book, her sweaty palm leaving prints on the binding.

Jane closed the book, its soft thud a call to action.

Begin with an adverb or article plus an adverb:

Jane closed the book, quickly fleeing the library.

Jane closed the diary, swiftly turning the key in its lock.

Begin with an article and a new proposition:

Jane closed the book, her hair sliding forward to hide her expression.

Jane closed the book, an hour wasted in fruitless research.

Begin with a base clause followed by a simile or metaphor that references the basic proposition:

Jane closed the book, sighing like a ghost.

Jane closed the diary, stealthy as a cat.

Revision Tips

✍ Read through your manuscript and examine each sentence. If you use a modifying phrase, make sure it does not contain both a subject and a verb and cannot stand alone. If it can stand alone, it should be a separate sentence.

✍ Does the modifying phrase modify part of the base clause: subject, verb, or object? If not, it doesn't belong there. It should be a separate sentence.

✍ Look for the word *as* and make sure you are not relating two actions at the same time that aren't physically possible.

PREPOSITIONS

Prepositions connect nouns, pronouns, and phrases with other words in a sentence. They give information about location, direction, space, and time. They are essential, but can be misused. If you overload a sentence with them, you make it hard to read. If you misplace them, you are creating a problem.

aboard	below	in	past
about	beneath	in front of	per
above	beside	inside	plus
absent	besides	instead of	regarding
across	between	into	round
after	beyond	like	save
against	but	mid	since
along	by	minus	than
alongside	concerning	near	through
amid	considering	next	till
amidst	despite	of	times
among	down	off	to
anti	during	on	toward
around	except	on top of	towards
as	excepting	onto	under
at	excluding	opposite	underneath
atop	following	out of	unlike
before	for	outside	until
behind	from	over	up

upon	via	within
versus	with	without

Revision Tips

✍ Do a search for prepositions by using [Control] [F] or Find. Is it used properly?

✍ Are there too many prepositions in the sentence?

✍ Can you cut the word and restructure the sentence?

VERB SELECTION

Without verbs, nothing would get done. The verb is the action part of the sentence. A subject performs the action.

Nouns and adjectives can be turned into verbs by adding the suffix *ify*, *ize*, *ate*, or *en*: deaden, digitize, fixate, immunize, originate, strategize, signify, sweeten.

Nouns and adjectives can be turned into verbs by adding the prefix *be*, *de*, or *en*: becalm, bedazzle, defrost, defrock, encompass, enmesh.

Made-up verbs have a suffix like *ify*, *ize*, *ate*, *en*, and *ing* added to them. It is important recognize when you are using made-up verbs. If you are, make sure they aren't a cliché, are intentional, and used only once or twice in a manuscript. Using it as a dialogue plant and payoff works. One lone character might mangle the language on purpose. Someone can mock him with it. Those are acceptable uses of imaginary verbs.

These suffixes create subtle speed bumps which force the reader to pause or reread the sentence. The suffix *ness* is often a substitute for a stronger word. This is where a thesaurus comes in handy.

Search for them. Read the sentence. Does it flow smoothly? Is the word out of place in your setting? Is it appropriate for the character to use it? Make sure words with these suffixes need to be there. If not, change them.

🖊 **Colorful verbs**: Avoid frequent use of verbs that are so colorful they distract. A little flowery wording in a manuscript is acceptable. Flowery wording in every paragraph isn't.

🖊 **Irregular verbs:** Most verbs are regular and are turned into past tense by adding *ed* or *en*. Irregular verbs do not follow this rule and include (in present, past, then past perfect order):

arise, arose, arisen
ask, asked, asked
attack, attacked, attacked
awaken, awakened/awoke awakened
bear, bore, borne/born
begin, began, begun
blow, blew, blown
break, broke, broken
bring, brought, brought
burst, burst, burst
choose, chose, chosen
cling, clung, clung
come, came, come
dive, dived/dove, dived
do, did, done
drag, dragged, dragged

draw, drew, drawn
drink, drank, drunk
drive, drove, driven
drown, drowned, drowned
eat, ate, eaten
fall, fell, fallen
fly, flew, flown
forgive, forgave, forgiven
freeze, froze, frozen
get, got, got/gotten
give, gave, given
go, went, gone
grow, grew, grown
hang (things), hung, hung
hang (people), hanged, hanged
happen, happened, happened
know, knew, known

lay, laid, laid
lead, led, led
lie, lay, lain
loosen, loosened, loosened
lose, lost, lost
pay, paid, paid
ride, rode, ridden
ring, rang, rung
rise, rose, risen
run, ran, run
see, saw, seen
set, set, set
shake, shook, shaken
shrink, shrank/shrunk, shrunk/shrunken
sing, sang, sung
sink, sank/sunk, sunk
sit, sat, sat
speak, spoke, spoken

spin, spun, spun
spit, spat, spat
spring, sprang/sprung, sprung
steal, stole, stolen
sting, stung, stung
stink, stank/stunk, stunk
strive, strove, striven
study, studied, studied
swear, swore, sworn
swim, swam, swum
swing, swung, swung
take, took, taken
tear, tore, torn
throw, threw, thrown
wake, woke/waked, woken/waked
wear, wore, worn
weave, wove, woven
wring, wrung, wrung
write, wrote, written

✎ **Passive verbs**: A single, active verb is more effective than passive verbs or passive verbs paired with adjectives. Search and kill as many passive verbs as you can. Look for: *am, is, are, was, were, being, be, been* and any verb ending in *ing*. A few passive verbs in a manuscript is fine; a few in a paragraph aren't.

Starting a phrase with a passive *ing* verb implies the two things happened simultaneously.

He danced, twirling plates on his head, singing a song.

He twirled plates on his head as he danced and sang.

Picking up her briefcase and locking the door, Sally rushed off to work.

Sally can't pick up her brief case, lock the door, and rush off to work all at the same time. The sentence should read:

Sally picked up her briefcase, locked the door then rushed to work.

If the items cannot happen simultaneously, change it.

✎ **Weak verbs**: Weak or simplistic verbs convey action but do not add further information. A verb that you had to modify with an adverb isn't a strong verb.

Weak: Sally ran fast.

Stronger: Sally sprinted.

Weak: Dick walked quietly into the room.

Stronger: Dick tiptoed into the room.

Weak: Jane hit the ball hard with the bat.

Stronger: Jane slammed the ball with the bat.

Revision Tips

✍ Do a Search and kill to remove as many passive and weak verbs as you can.

✍ Look at the verb in each sentence. Is it doing its job properly?

✍ Do the subject and verb agree?

✍ Look for suspect suffixes: *ness, ize, ly, ing,* and *ingly.* Can you cut it or exchange it for a stronger word?

Diana Hurwitz

VERB TENSE &

SPLIT INFINITIVES

Verb tense cues the reader in to *when* an action took place. Verb tenses should change only when there is a change in time.

In terms of story structure, there are only two specific tenses to worry about: present and past.

It most commercial fiction, the stories are written in what is considered *past tense*. That doesn't mean a sentence cannot use a different tense if required. Rather, the story is related as if it had already happened and the reader is only now learning about it from the point of view character.

Stories written in present tense are less common and relate the story as if it is happening right at that very moment to the point of view character. Writing an entire novel in present tense is tricky.

A story could be told in present tense with a backstory told in past tense. If not done consistently, or expertly, it will alienate the reader.

The rest of the complex verb forms are marked by words called auxiliaries. Grasping the six basic tenses allows a writer to control the timeframe of the scenes through the sentence structure.

🕐 **Simple Present**: We write (we are writing right now).

🕐 **Present Perfect**: We have written (we just finished writing).

🕐 **Simple Past**: We wrote (we wrote in the past).

🕐 **Past Perfect**: We had written (we wrote in the distant past).

🕐 **Future**: We will write (we will write at some future date).

🕐 **Future Perfect**: We will have written (in retrospect, we will have written at some future date).

Problems in sequencing tenses tend to occur with the perfect tenses, all of which are formed by adding words to the past participles: *had, have, will,* and *will have.* The most common add-ons are: *be, can, do, has, have, had, may, must, ought, shall, will,* and *would.*

Verb tense alerts you to narrator intrusions.

Sally didn't understand yet that her life <u>would</u> never be the same.

Aside from poor foreshadowing, if you've been using past tense, you just launched the reader into a future timeframe.

Let's review verb tenses in detail.

🕐**Present tense:** When using present tense, the verb choice reflects an unchanging, repeated, or reoccurring action or situation that exists in the present. Few stories are written in present tense.

I stroke his hair.

His hand slides down my arm, his thumb searching for a pulse.

🕐 **Present progressive tense** describes an ongoing action that is happening at the same time the statement is written. This tense is formed by using *am, is, are* with the verb form ending in *ing*.

I am stroking his hair.

We are walking the dog.

The sun is shining.

🕐 **Present perfect tense** refers to something that happened at an indefinite time in the past or that began in the past and continues into the present. It uses *have* or *had* in combination with the past participle of the verb, usually ending in *ed*. Irregular verbs have special past participles.

We have searched high and low and cannot find it.

We have been using this process for five years.

🕐 **Present perfect progressive tense** describes an action that began in the past, continues in the present, and may continue into the future. This tense is formed by using *has* and *have been* and the present participle of the verb ending in *ing*.

We have been considering the possibility of retiring to Florida.

🕐 **Past Tense**

When using past tense, the verb choice expresses an action or situation that started and finished in the past and usually ends in *ed*. Irregular verbs have special past tense forms. Most commercial fiction is written in past tense.

Sally reached for the knife.

Dick raced down the stairs.

I led the charge into the building.

🕐 **Past progressive tense** is used to describe a past action which was happening when another action occurred and uses *was* and *were* with a verb ending in *ing*.

I was reaching for his knife.

Dick was racing down the stairs when the alarm sounded.

This tense is considered passive and writers are encouraged to do a search and kill for sentences using *was* plus *ing*. Try searching for the word *was* in your draft. It will take hours, but do it. Get rid of as many as you can.

🕐 **Past perfect tense** is used for an action that took place in the past before another past action. This tense is formed by using *had* with the past participle of the verb.

By the time we arrived, the fight had ended.

🕐 **Past perfect progressive tense** references a past but ongoing action that was completed before some other past action. This tense is formed by using *had been* and the present perfect form of the verb ending in *ing*.

Before the alarm rang, the firemen had been cooking dinner and playing poker.

⏱ **Future Tense**

Future tense expresses a situation that has not yet occurred. It uses *will* or *shall.*

Dick will go the store on Monday.

Jane shall meet the deadline.

⏱ **Progressive future tense** describes an ongoing or continuous action that will take place in the future. This tense is formed by using *will be* or *shall be* with a verb ending in *ing.*

Jane will be singing with the choir on July fourth.

⏱ **Future perfect tense** refers to an action that will occur in the future before some other action. This tense is formed by using *will have* with the past participle of the verb.

By the time we arrive in London, the tour bus will have been waiting there for several days.

⏱ **Future perfect progressive tense** refers to a future, ongoing action that will occur before some specified future time, using *will have been* and the present participle of verbs ending in *ing.*

By this time next year, we will have been publishing and selling more books than we ever imagined.

Shifting viewpoint does not mean shifting tense. If you are attributing thoughts to a character, you do not shift into the present tense to express them unless you are writing the piece in present tense.

Incorrect: "I really hate them," she <u>thinks</u>.

Correct: "I really hate them," she <u>thought.</u>

Shifting tense and misuse of tense are plot holes. They are hard to ignore and interrupt the flow. It forces the reader to re-read a sentence or paragraph. Subtle, unintended time shifts create confusion. A reader might have to stop and ask, *"Did he or will he?"*

Another thing to keep in mind with verb usage is variety. Sitting, standing, running, jumping, sighing, weeping, and laughing are all fine when used moderately. Finding a fresh way to say them or using a greater variety of verbs makes the story richer. You can find lists of verbs on the internet. I have a list of basic verbs and replacements for them that I add to constantly. This is a good revision layer. Do a document search or underline common verbs in your draft and see how many you can change into something stronger.

There is a difference between passive voice and past tense. Past tense means the action already occurred. Passive voice has to do with who did or did not do something. It almost always includes forms of the verb *to be*. In active voice, the subject does something. In the passive voice, something is done to the subject.

It is generally considered better to use active rather than passive verbs. In the revision phase, as you read the sentences, identify the subject and verb. Does the subject of the verb perform the action of the main verb or does he sit there while something or someone else performs the action? If the subject performs the verb, it is active. If it doesn't, it's passive.

Passive: The victim was drowned around midnight.

Active: The murderer drowned the victim around midnight.

Passive: Jane was scratched by Puff.

Active: Puff scratched Jane.

In instances when the writer does not know the *doer* of the verb, the *doer* is not important, or there are many *doers*, it is acceptable to use passive verbs. If you are intentionally obscuring *whodunit*, you might say, "*Dick was murdered.*" If you say, "*It was just lying there,*" you have indicated that it doesn't matter who left it lying there or why.

A character might always speak passively as a quirk.

Linking verbs indicate a state of being, not action: *is, was, are, seems, becomes.*

Passive verbs and modifiers shouldn't be mixed. If you begin a sentence with a modifying phrase, it becomes a dangling modifier if you follow it with a passive verb.

Sighing softly, the book was placed on the table.

The sentence forgot to mention who sighed and placed the book on the table. Supplying the missing *who* turns it into an active sentence.

Sighting softly, Jane placed the book on the table.

Jane sighed softly and placed the book on the table.

The infinitive of a verb is its basic form with or without the particle *to*: *do/to do* and *be/to be*.

An infinitive verb almost always begins with *to* followed by the simple form of the verb.

Dick likes <u>to run</u> often.

Dick wants <u>to fly</u> planes.

Dick used <u>to walk</u> to work.

An infinitive is not a verb. Don't add *s, es, ed,* or *ing* to the end. Infinitives can be used as nouns, adjectives, or adverbs.

A split infinitive is inserting a word between *to* and the verb.

Incorrect: Sally wanted to thoroughly kiss him.

Correct: Sally wanted to kiss him thoroughly.

For effect: Sally wanted to kiss him, thoroughly.

This rule is broken frequently. If you choose to split infinitives, do it intentionally and for emphasis, not because you don't understand the rule.

Revision Tips

✍ Read through your manuscript. What verb tense are you using? Is it consistent?

✍ Are you using the tenses correctly?

✍ Highlight thoughts, dreams, and asides. Are you using consistent verb tense throughout?

✍ How many times have you used *was* or *were* with verbs ending in *ing*?

✍ Have you created time shifts or narrator intrusions?

✍ Have you split infinitives? Change it unless you used it sparingly for effect.

SUBJECT VERB AGREEMENT

When revising, it is important to look at each sentence for subject verb agreement. This is one of those skills that come naturally over time. There are a few tricky circumstances that you may sometimes need to double check.

A singular subject requires a singular verb. A plural subject requires a plural verb with a few exceptions.

I <u>sing</u>. You <u>sing</u>. We all <u>sing</u> for ice cream.

The little girls all <u>sang</u> for their supper.

If the subject has two singular nouns joined with *and* use a plural verb.

Dick and Jane <u>are</u> ready to go home.

If the subject has two singular nouns joined with *or* or *nor*, use a singular verb.

Neither Dick nor Jane <u>is</u> ready to go home.

If the subject has a singular noun joined to a plural noun by *or* or *nor*, the verb should agree with whichever noun comes last.

Neither Dick nor his friends <u>want</u> to play catch outside.

Either Sally or Jane visits everyday.

The contractions *doesn't* (*does not*) and *wasn't* (*was not*) are always used with a singular subject.

Dick <u>doesn't</u> want to go.

The contractions *don't* (*do not*) and *weren't* (*were not*) are always used with a plural subject. The exception to this rule is *I* and *you* require *don't*.

We don't want to go with Jane.

You don't believe me.

I don't want to go home yet.

When a modifying phrase comes between the subject and the verb, it does not change the agreement. The verb always agrees with the subject, not the modifying phrase.

Dick, as well as his friends, <u>hopes</u> the Colts win.

Jane, as well as Sally and Dick, <u>hopes</u> the meeting will be over soon.

Distributives are singular and need a singular verb: *anybody, anyone, each, each one, either, everybody, everyone, neither, no, one, nobody, somebody, someone.*

Each of them will go there someday.

Nobody knows Dick is here.

Either way works.

Neither option is viable.

Plural nouns functioning as a single unit, such as *mathematics, measles,* and *mumps,* require singular verbs. An exception is the word *dollars.* When used to reference an amount of money, *dollars* requires a singular verb; but when referring to the bills themselves, a plural verb is required.

Five thousand dollars would suffice.

Dollars are easier to exchange than Euros.

Another exception is nouns with two parts. They can usually be prefaced with *a pair of* and require a plural verb: *glasses, pants, panties, scissors,* or *trousers.* Why they are considered pairs is another question.

Dick's trousers are worn.

Jane's scissors are missing.

When a sentence begins with the verb phrases *there is* and *there are* and is followed by the subject, the verb must agree with the subject that follows.

There are many who would agree with you.

There is the question of who goes first.

A subject can be modified by a phrase that begins with: *accompanied by, as well as, as with, in addition to, including,* or *together with.* However, this does not modify the plurality of the subject. If the subject is single, it requires a singular verb. If the subject is plural, it requires a plural verb.

Dick, accompanied by his wife Jane, will arrive in ten minutes.

Everything, including the kitchen sink, is up for auction.

The cousins, together with their dog, are going to be here for a week.

Revision Tips

✍ This step needs to be done sentence by sentence and is best done on a printed copy. Identify the complicated sentences.

✍ Underline the subject and verb. Do they agree? If not, correct them.

✍ Make sure the modifying phrases are used correctly.

Diana Hurwitz

VERB PHRASES

The section reviews a verb's purpose and explains what a verb phrase is. A verb tells the reader what happens. The action can be modified by an object, assisted with a helper, or modified by a verb phrase. Verb phrases are often used in idioms, colloquialisms, or slang.

A verb object is the item upon which the action is committed.

Jane drove (subject/verb) the car (object).

Dick threw (subject/verb) the ball (object).

A verb can be modified with a *helping* verb:

Forms of *to be*: am, are, be, been, is, was, were.

Forms of *to do*: did, do, does.

Forms of *to have*: had, has, have.

Qualifiers: can, could, may, might, shall, should, will, would.

A verb can be modified by a verb phrase. A verb phrase contains a verb and a helping verb that act as one word. The helping word always precedes the verb. The words *never*, *not*, and the contraction *n't* are negation words and are not part of the verb.

Dick <u>could have been willing</u> (verb) to fly (modifier).

Dick <u>might</u> not <u>have wanted</u> (verb) to fly (modifier)

We <u>have become </u>(verb) world travelers (object).

The helping verb can be separated from the verb in certain situations. When asking a question, the helping verb comes before the actual verb.

<u>Have</u> you ever <u>been</u> to Spain?

<u>Do</u> you <u>know</u> the way to San Jose?

No, I'<u>ve</u> never <u>been</u> there.

Dick <u>should</u> never (negation) <u>have gone (verb)</u> there (modifier).

Revision Tips

✍ Make sure the verb phrases are used correctly. You should search for these verb phrase key words by selecting [Control] [F] or [Find] and entering the word. Make sure you avoid clichés.

✍ Evaluate all verb phrases. Are they used correctly?

✍ Do they constitute clichés? Can you change it or cut it?

Diana Hurwitz

ADVERBS, MODIFIERS & NEGATION

Some critics would like to see all adverbs die slowly and painfully. Others believe there is room for them if used sparingly and not as a dialogue tag. In the preceding sentences, I used three of them effectively. You can too. Use them deliberately instead of out of laziness.

✎ Adverbs should not be used at the beginning of a sentence to introduce an idea. This rule was made to be broken because people do speak that way. Do it judiciously in your dialogue, not incorrectly by accident.

"<u>Generally</u>, I'd <u>disagree</u> with you," Dick said.

Adverbs should modify a verb or other adverb.

"I'd <u>generally disagree</u> with you," Dick said.

I don't <u>usually go</u> out with strangers.

🖉 Negation uses words that change an affirmative statement into a denial statement.

cannot	does not	neither	should not
can't	doesn't	no	shouldn't
could not	has not	nor	was not
couldn't	hasn't	not	wasn't
do not	have not	shall not	would not
don't	haven't	shan't	wouldn't.

Not, neither, nor, and *no* can be used to negate both nouns and verbs.

Your excuse is neither here nor there.

Jane was not home.

No man is an island.

It's not that I don't like him; I don't trust him.

The exception is the verb *do* which must be repeated to negate something.

Puff does not do tricks.

🖉 Double negatives should be avoided unless used judiciously to illustrate character or to be intentionally cagey.

Incorrect: Dick don't have no sense.

Correct: Dick has no sense.

Incorrect: Nobody doesn't like Sarah Lee.

Correct: Everyone likes Sarah Lee.

Correct: Dick didn't *disagree* with Jane's suggestion.

🖉 Not all adverbs end in *ly*. Some modify how something is done in a slightly different way. You don't have to cut modifiers out entirely, but you should sprinkle them throughout a manuscript. If you dump the same word several times on the same page, cut it down to once. This is hard, especially if you write the way you talk, because it sounds correct. My personal nemesis is "*just*." I have a tendency to use it in every other sentence. The more clutter you can get rid of, the tighter your sentences will be.

Explanation:	Frequency:	Location:	Time:
almost	always	abroad	after
because	every	anywhere	afterwards
end up	less	downstairs	already
even	more	everywhere	during
in order to	never	here	finally
not	often	home	just
kind of	rarely	in	last
mostly	seldom	nowhere	later
quite	sometimes	out	next
seemed	usually	outside	now
since		somewhere	recently
so		there	soon
so that		underground	then
sort of		upright	tomorrow
to		upside-down	when
try		upstairs	while
very		upward	yesterday

✎ For adverbs that do end in *ly*, do a search and see how often they are used. Cut each adverb down to once or twice per manuscript. Add your favorites to the list. When you use them, do so for impact and with intention.

A cumulative sentence and dialogue are good places to have them. After a dialogue tag is not.

"If you have adverbs as dialogue tags, cut them," the editor insisted petulantly.

"Unless you completely disagree with the rule," the writer argued vociferously.

I can't list all adverbs, but I offer some of the most common.

A
abnormally
absentmindedly
absolutely
accidentally
acidly
actually
adventurously
angrily
annually
anxiously
arrogantly
awkwardly

B
badly
bashfully
beautifully
bitterly
bleakly

blindly
blissfully
boastfully
boldly
bravely
briefly
brightly
briskly
broadly
busily

C
calmly
carefully
carelessly
cautiously
certainly
cheerfully
clearly
cleverly

closely
coaxingly
colorfully
commonly
completely
continually
constantly
continuously
coolly
correctly
courageously
crossly
cruelly
curiously

D
daily
daintily
dearly
deceivingly

delightfully
deeply
defiantly
deliberately
delightfully
diligently
dimly
doubtfully
dreamily

E

eagerly
easily
elegantly
energetically
enormously
enthusiastically
equally
especially
evenly
eventually
exactly
excitedly

F

fairly
faithfully
famously
far
fast
fatally
ferociously
fervently
fiercely
finally
fondly
foolishly
fortunately
frankly

frantically
freely
frenetically
frightfully
fully
furiously

G

generally
generously
gently
gladly
gleefully
gracefully
gratefully
greatly
greedily

H

happily
hastily
healthfully
heavily
helpfully
helplessly
highly
honestly
hopefully
hopelessly
hotly
hourly
hungrily

I

inconceivably
incredibly
immediately
innocently
inquisitively

instantly
intensely
intently
interestingly
inwardly
ironically
irritably

J

jaggedly
jealously
jokingly
joyfully
joyously
jovially
jubilantly
judgmentally
justly

K

keenly
kiddingly
kindheartedly
kindly
knavishly
knowingly
knowledgably

L

lazily
liberally
lightly
likely
limply
literally
lively
loftily
longingly
loosely

lovingly
loudly
loyally
lustfully

M
madly
majestically
meaningfully
mechanically
merrily
miserably
mockingly
monthly
mortally
mostly
mournfully
mysteriously

N
naturally
nearly
neatly
nervously
never
nicely
nimbly
noisily

O
obediently
obnoxiously
oddly
offensively
officially
only
openly
optimistically
overconfidently

owlishly

P
painfully
partially
patiently
perfectly
physically
playfully
politely
poorly
positively
potentially
powerfully
prominently
prolifically
promptly
properly
punctually

Q
quaintly
queasily
queerly
questionably
questioningly
quicker
quickly
quietly
quirkily
quixotically
quizzically

R
rapidly
rarely
readily
really
reassuringly

recklessly
regularly
reluctantly
repeatedly
reproachfully
restfully
righteously
rightfully
rigidly
roughly
rudely

S
sadly
safely
scarcely
scarily
searchingly
sedately
seemingly
selfishly
separately
seriously
shakily
sharply
sheepishly
shrilly
shyly
silently
sleepily
slowly
smoothly
softly
solemnly
solidly
soulfully
speedily
stealthily
sternly

strictly
successfully
suddenly
surprisingly
suspiciously
sweetly
swiftly
sympathetically

T
tenderly
tensely
terribly
thankfully
thoroughly
thoughtfully
tightly
tomorrow
totally
too
tremendously
triumphantly
truly
truthfully

U
ultimately
unabashedly
unaccountably

unbearably
unethically
unexpectedly
unfortunately
unimpressively
unnaturally
unnecessarily
utterly
upbeat
upwardly
urgently
usefully
uselessly
usually
utterly

V
vaguely
vainly
valiantly
vastly
verbally
very
viciously
victoriously
violently
vivaciously
voluntarily

W
warmly
weakly
wearily
well
wetly
wholly
wildly
willfully
wisely
woefully
wonderfully
worriedly
wrongly

Y
yawningly
yearly
yearningly
yesterday
yieldingly
youthfully

Z
zealously
zestfully

Revision Tips

✍ Go down the list. Add your favorites. Do a search and kill. Reword the sentence without the adverb. The sentence should work if you cut it. To do a search hit [Control] [F] and Highlight All or Find Next. Save frequently using [Control] [S].

✍ Are you choosing adverbs over strong verbs? If so, choose stronger verbs.

✍ If you keep adverbs, make sure they are in the right place and serving a distinct purpose.

✍ If you disagree with the adverb rule, make sure you are not descending into purple prose or clichés. Make sure you find an editor that says, "Adverbs are delightful, use them prominently and prolifically."

✍ Have you used double negatives? Correct them unless you used them for effect.

CONJUNCTIONS, CORRELATIVES

& TRANSITIONS

Connectives and transitions string ideas together in a sentence.

✎ Conjunctions serve as a trailer hitch that joins two sentences together. In general, you should not begin a sentence with a conjunction. It is sometimes acceptable if what follows the conjunction is an independent clause with a subject and verb. If not, the clause is considered a sentence fragment. This rule is often broken in the name of *style*.

Dick wanted to find Jane. And he didn't.

The seasons change. And so do I.

The key is to not overuse this tactic or do it in error. You will be viewed as a rookie rather than stylish. In fiction, you should avoid making the sentences sound too clinical or formal without murdering the language.

Conjunctions can become repetitive words. Make sure each conjunction does not appear in every other sentence.

When two words or phrases are joined by a conjunction, no comma is needed.

Dick ran and Sally walked.

When two or more items are listed before a conjunction, those items should be separated by commas:

Dick, wearing a hat, gloves, and a scarf, dashed outside to play in the snow.

When two complete sentences are joined by a conjunction, you should generally place a comma before the conjunction.

The moon waxes and wanes, and the sun rises and sets, and mankind lives and dies.

This rule is broken stylistically in rhetorical devices and cumulative sentences.

Dick hated leaving and he hated staying and he wished the move was behind him.

Dick hated leaving. He hated staying. He wished the move was behind him.

You can see how stringing the short sentences together with conjunctions gave it punch.

Adding

also	beside	moreover
and	furthermore	too
as well as	in addition	

Cause and effect

as	now that	thus
as a result	since	while
because	so	why
consequently	so that	
in order that	therefore	

Compare

accordingly	equally	likewise
as with	in the same way	similarly
compared with	like	

Contrast

alternatively	however	though
although	in contrast	unlike
but	instead of	whereas
conversely	on the other hand	while
even though	otherwise	

Emphasis

above all	in particular	notably
especially	indeed	rather
furthermore	moreover	significantly so
hence	most of all	

Illustrating

as revealed by	for example	such as
assuming that	for instance	
even if	in the case of	

Qualifying

although	if	thus
apart from	in case	unless
as long as	nevertheless	until
assuming that	only if	when
but	providing that	where
despite	since	wherever
even if	still	whether or not
except for	then	yet
however	therefore	

Sequencing

as	next	then
after	once	third
before	second	while
finally	since	why
first	so	
meanwhile	that	

🖋 Correlatives are words that are separated in a sentence, but work together. Correlatives link balanced words, phrases, and clauses. The elements connected by correlative conjunctions are usually parallel, that is, similar in length and grammatical form.

Coordinating correlatives give equal weight to both clauses:

as ___, as

both ___, and

either ___, or

just as ___, so

228

neither ___, nor

not only ___, but also

the more ___, the less

the more ___, the more

no sooner ___, than

so ___, as

whether ___, or

Subordinating correlatives indicate that one clause is less important than the other:

if ___, then

less ___, than

more ___, than

so ___, that

Reference the section on cumulative sentences for how to use them well.

Transitions bridge separate ideas, sentences, and paragraphs. Transition phrases can be used to add, change location, change time, clarify, compare, conclude, emphasize, or summarize.

Use them with care. Search for overuse. A few times in a chapter is fine. A few times in a paragraph is not.

Addition

additionally	even more	further	second
again	important	furthermore	secondly
along with	equally	in addition	thirdly
also	finally	in the second	together with
and	first	place	too
another	firstly	likewise	
as well	for example	moreover	
besides	for instance	next	

Change Location

above	away from	here	on top of
across	back of	in front of	opposite
adjacent to	behind	inside	outside
against	beneath	into	over
along	beside	near	throughout
alongside	between	off	to the right
amid	beyond	onto	to the left
among	by	on the	under
around	down	opposite side	

Change Time

about	eventually	presently
after	finally	prior to
afterward	first	second
as soon as	immediately	soon thereafter
at	in the meantime	third
at length	in the past	till
at once	later	today
after a few days	meanwhile	tomorrow
before	next	until then
consequently	next week	when
during	now	yesterday

Clarify

for example	in other words	to clarify
for instance	stated differently	
for this purpose	that is	

Compare

although	even though	like
as	for instance	likewise
as if	furthermore	nevertheless
as opposed to	however	on the contrary
at the same time	in addition	on the other hand
but	in contrast	otherwise
conversely	in like manner	similarly
counter to	in spite of	still
even if	in the same way	too
even so	instead	yet

Conclude or Summarize

accordingly	finally	on the whole
all in all	in brief	therefore
as a result	in conclusion	thus
consequently	in short	to sum up
due to	in summary	

Emphasize

again	in fact	to emphasize
as has been noted	indeed	to illustrate
for the reason	that is	to repeat
in any event	thus	to sum up
in other words	to be sure	truly

Revision Tips

✍ Do a search using [Control] [F] or Find. Is the word used correctly?

✍ How often is the connector used? Do you need to reduce the number of times you used it?

✍ Make sure the word is performing the appropriate function.

✍ Does it add to the meaning of the sentence or obscure it?

CLICHÉS, IDIOMS & PURPLE PROSE

✎ **Clichés** are overused metaphors and often employ the words *like* and *as*. Agents and editors hate clichés. However, clichés are so deeply imbedded in our language, we don't know we are using them. Personally, I applaud all those creative people who came up with the phrases that give our language its biting wit, sappy compliments, colorful swear words, and delightful put downs. Our world would be boring without them.

Detractors call clichés predictable, annoying, a symptom of lazy writing, and bordering on purple prose. The main concern is cliché abuse.

✎ **Idioms** are colloquial metaphors. They say one thing but mean another and cannot be taken literally. If a couple breaks up, that means they stop seeing each other, not that body parts go flying. There are thousands of idioms that enrich our language. The trouble begins when a child, foreign person, or alien takes one of our idioms literally. "*We'll have you for dinner,*" does not mean the person will be eaten by cannibals.

There isn't room to list the busload of idioms, but here are a few examples:

at length	in step with	run along
burn off	lay aside	slap on the wrist
by the way	leaf through	take a lick at
chin up	no less than	think tank
common touch	put down	
fly away	put in the way of	

🖉 **Purple prose** consists of passages of prose so cloying, over the top, or dramatic that they create speed bumps for the reader. It employs an abundance of adjectives and dense descriptive detail. Purple prose should be weeded out when found, unless that is your preferred writing style. In which case, you may deter some readers and agents. The worst offenders are romantic scenes, because writers try to avoid clinical terms for the acts of love and body parts. A lot of slang words are too crude and don't fit the mood of the piece. Purple prose can be a product of weak description writing. Some writers stuff so many descriptions in a paragraph the reader forgets the topic.

Avoid using things like: bated breath (not baited!), cupid lips, framed by, heart-shaped face, limped pools, manly chin, revealed, set off by, steely eyes, heaving or swelling bosom, tumescent member, and wriggling eyebrows.

Avoid melodramatic descriptions such as:

Her ample bosom heaved as he slowly untied her frilled, satin night dress. His caress made her tremble like a delicate blossom in the breeze as he nibbled on the petals of her ears.

Enough said. The key to using clichés well is to use them sparingly and to twist them to make them original. They can be placed strategically to add a comic punch or to define a single character, not the entire cast.

Cliché: Dick won't rock the boat.

Twist: Dick won't rock the rescue dinghy.

Cliché: Not for all the tea in China.

Twist: Not for all the fortune cookies in China.

There are too many clichés to list them all here, but I offer examples. Some are so ingrained in our language, it would sound stilted to avoid them. Make artistic choices.

A

abandon ship
about face
above board
absence makes the heart grow fonder
absolute power corrupts absolutely
ace in the hole
ace up his sleeve
Achilles heel
acid test
actions speak louder than words
after my own heart
airing dirty laundry
all bent out of shape
all bets are off
all dressed up and nowhere to go

all ears
all for one and one for all
all hands on deck
all hell breaks loose
all in a day's work
all in due time
all over the map
all pales in comparison
all talk no action
all that glitters is not gold
all that jazz
all thumbs
all work and no play
all wet
all's fair in love and war
all's well that ends well
always a bridesmaid
an apple a day
an arm and a leg
an idle mind is the devil's playground
an oldie but goodie
an ounce of prevention is worth a pound of cure
another day another dollar
ants in his pants
any port in a storm
anyhoo
anything goes
apple of my eye
armed to the teeth
around the horn
as all get out
as the day is long
as far as the eye can see
as good as gold
as honest as the day is long
as if
as luck would have it

as plain as the nose on your face
as snug as a bug in a rug
as the crow flies
as useful as a lead balloon
ashes to ashes dust to dust
ask me no questions
asleep at the wheel
ass backwards
at the crack of dawn
at the drop of a hat
at the eleventh hour
at the end of my rope
at the end of the day
at the last minute
at wits' end
atta boy
atta girl
axe to grind

B

babe in the woods
baby blues
baby boomer
back against the wall
back breaking
back from the dead
backhanded compliment
back in a sec
back in the saddle
back it up
back seat driver
back stabber
back to square one
back to the drawing board
bad wrap
bad blood
bad call
bad hair day

bad seed
bad to the bone
bag and baggage
bait and switch
baked
baker's dozen
bald-faced liar
ball is in your court
ball of wax
bang your head against a brick wall
bank on it
baptism by fire
bare bones
barge right in
barking up the wrong tree
barn burner
basket case
bat the idea around
bats in the belfry
be in the same boat
be there or be square
bear down
beat a dead horse
beat around the bush
beat it
beats me
bee in her bonnet
been there done that
bee's knees
beggars can't be choosers
behind the eight ball
behind the times
belle of the ball
bells and whistles
bend over backwards
best laid plans
best thing since sliced bread
bet it all

bet the farm
bet your bottom dollar
better half
better late than never
better safe than sorry
better than ever
better the Devil you know than the Devil you don't
between a rock and a hard place
bigger than life
big brother is watching
bigger they are the harder they fall
biological clock is ticking
birds of a feather
bite me
bite off more than you can chew
bite the bullet
bit the dust
bit your lip
bite your tongue
black as pitch
black eye
black Friday
blast from the past
blaze a new trail
blew him away
blind as a bat
blind leading the blind
blood is thicker than water
blood money
bloom is off the rose
blow a gasket
blow the whistle on
blow this joint
blow your brains out
blowing smoke up my ass

blue Monday
body is still warm
body slam
boils down to
bombed
bone-chilling cold
bone of contention
bone to pick
bone up on
bored to tears
born with a silver spoon in his mouth
both barrels
both feet on the ground
bottom fell out
bottom line
bottom out
bought the farm
bounce back
bowl someone over
box yourself in
boy howdy
boys will be boys
bragging rights
brain drain
brain dump
bread winner
break a leg
break ranks
break the ice
bring home the bacon
bring it
bring it on
brown nose
brush off
buck naked
buck stops here
buckle down
build a better mousetrap

built like a brick shithouse
bum steer
bump on a log
bun in the oven
burn the candle at both ends
burn the midnight oil
burn your bridges
bury the hatchet
business as usual
business at hand
bust your balls
bust your chops
busted
busted a gut
busy as a bee
butterflies in his stomach
buy in to
buy something for a song
by the book
by the same token

C

caca me me scheme
call a spade a spade
call it a day
call off the dogs
call on the carpet
call the shots
can it
can of whoop ass
can of worms
can't have your cake and eat it too
can't hold a candle
can't judge a book by its cover
can't teach an old dog new tricks
carry the team
cash cow

cash in your chips
cash is king
cash it in
cast a long shadow
cat got your tongue
cat nap
catch my drift
catch a falling star
catch forty winks
catch on
catching some ZZZ's
cat's meow
cat's whiskers
caught me off guard
caught with his pants down
champagne taste and a beer budget
change your tune
changes hands
chatty Cathy
cheap date
cheap shot
cheap trick
chew on
chew out
chew the fat
chief cook and bottle washer
child's play
chill out
chip in
chip off the old block
chip on your shoulder
chomping at the bit
clean bill of health
clean sweep
clean your clock
clear as a bell
clear as mud
clear the air

climb the walls
clock is ticking
close call
close early and often
close ranks
clue me in
coast to coast
cock and bull story
coin a phrase
cold as ice
cold feet
cold shoulder
collared
come across
come again
come hell or high water
come in under the wire
come out of the closet
coming down in buckets
complete picture
cookie cutter
cool as a cucumber
cool your heels
cool your jets
cop it
cover my ass
cowboy up
crack down
crack the code
crack the nut
crack the whip
cracking up
crap shoot
crazy as a loon
crazy like a fox
cream of the crop
crime doesn't pay
crocodile tears
cross the line

cry all the way to the bank
cry me a river
cry over spilled milk
cry uncle
cry wolf
curb your enthusiasm
curiosity killed the cat
cut a rug
cut and dried
cut corners
cut it out
cut off your nose to spite your face
cut the cheese
cut the mustard
cut to the chase
cut your losses
cut your teeth on
cute as a button
cuts like a knife
cuts to the core
cuts to the quick

D
dagger (knife) in the heart
damned if you do and damned if you don't
dances to the beat of a different drum
dark horse
day late and a dollar short
dead as a doornail
dead cat bounce
dead presidents
dead ringer
dead to rights
deal with it
dealt a fatal blow
death by a thousand cuts

deep do do
deep six something
deer in the headlights
diamond in the rough
dig for gold
dirt cheap
do a one-eighty
do as I say not as I do
do birds fly
do or die
do what it takes
do you feel me
doesn't have a prayer
doesn't stand a chance
dog eat dog
dog's life
doing time
don't bite the hand that feeds you
don't count your chickens
don't do anything I wouldn't do
don't go there
don't have two nickels to rub together
don't hold your breath
don't know him from Adam
don't look a gift horse in the mouth
don't rock the boat
don't shoot me
don't sweat it
don't tempt fate
double whammy
down and out
down in the mouth
down on your luck
down the hatch
draw a blank
dream on

dressed to kill
dressed to the nines
drink the Kool-Aid
drive me to drink
drive me nuts
drive me up a wall
drive me crazy
drop a dime
drop in the bucket
drop me a line
dropping like flies
drown your sorrows
drunk as a skunk
dry as a bone
dumb as a fox
dumb as a post
dumb as a stump
dumber than a bag of hammers
dumber than a box of rocks
Dutch treat

E

early bird catches the worm.
early to bed and early to rise
easy as 123
easy as ABC
easy as pie
eat crow
eat lead
eat like a horse
eat my hat
eat your gun
eat your own dog food
elephant in the room
emotional roller coaster
empty flattery
end over end
ends justify the means

even keeled
even money
even Stevens
every dog has his day
everything but the kitchen sink
everything's coming up roses
everything's copasetic
everything's hunky dory
eye for an eye tooth for a tooth
eyeball someone or something

F

face only a mother could love
faint heart
fair haired one
fair weather friend
fall guy
fall head over heels
fall through the cracks
falling off a log
family affair
fan the flames
fancy meeting you here
far cry
fast buck
fat as a cow
fat as a pig
fat chance
feather in his cap
federal case
fell off my plate
few bricks shy
few fries short of a happy meal
few sandwiches short of a picnic
fickle finger of fate
fifty-fifty
fight like cats and dogs
figure it out

filthy rich
fine and dandy
fine as wine
fine line
fingered
firing on all cylinders
first things first
fish or cut bait
fish out of water
fit as a fiddle
fit to be hung
fit to be tied
fits like a glove
flash in the pan
flat as a board
flat as a pancake
fleet footed
flew the coop
fling
flip flop
flip your lid
flog a dead horse
fly by night
fly by the book
fly by the seat of your pants
fly in the ointment
fly on the wall
follow the leader
following in his footsteps
fool and his money are soon parted
fool's gold
for crying out loud
for Pete's sake
forever and a day
fork it over
fork out
free as a bird
free reign

frog in a frying pan
frog in my throat
from day one
full of herself
full of himself
full of hot air
full of mischief
funny business
fur coat and no knickers
fur fly

Ⓖ
gadzooks
gang bang
garlic milkshake
get the ball rolling
get a life
get a room
get a word in edgewise
get all worked up
get an earful
get back up on the horse
get cleaned out
get crushed
get down
get it
get lost
get the message
get off
get out of my hair
get over the hump
get off the hook
get to the bottom of it
get with the program
get your feet wet
get your foot in the door
getting hitched
give a hoot
give and take

give it a rest
give it a whirl
give it away
give me a hand
give the shirt off your back
give them a hand
give them an inch
give your right arm
glimmer of hope
gloss over
glutton for punishment
go against the grain
go back to the well
go ballistic
go belly up
go down hill
go figure
go fly a kite
go for broke
go head to head
go jump in the lake
go out in a blaze of glory
go out on a limb
go over his head
go overboard
go postal
go the extra mile
go through the motions
go through the roof
go too far
go with your gut
going bananas
going gang-busters
gold digger
golden child
good call
good man is hard to find
good rule of thumb
good soldier

good things come to those who
wait
good to go
good to the last drop
goofing off
got a leg up
got burned
got off on the wrong foot
got your nose out of joint
grasping at straws
grass is always greener on the
other side
grease a palm
green-eyed monster
green horn
green with envy
greener pastures
grey hairs
grin and bear it
grinning from ear to ear
ground rules
groundhog day
growing like a weed
gunning for
guns blazing
gut check

[H]
half a bubble off
half-baked idea
hammered
hand off
handle it with kid gloves
hands on
handwriting on the wall
hang in there
hang me out to dry
hang on every word
hang yourself

happy as a clam
happy as a lark
happy camper
hard day's night
hard headed
hard stop
hard to swallow
hare-brained idea
has a leg up
haste makes waste
hat in hand
hate his guts
have a cow
have a heart
have a heart attack
have a nice day
have a shot
have a stick up your ass
have the last laugh
he is toast
he learned his lesson
he never met a doughnut he didn't like
he who laughs last laughs best
he's got game
head over heels
heads up
heard it through the grapevine
heart breaker
heart of gold
heart of stone
heaven help us
hell in a hand basket
hell raiser
hen pecked
here today gone tomorrow
high as a kite
high hopes
high maintenance

highway robbery
hindsight is twenty/twenty
his bark is worse than his bite
history repeats itself
hit below the belt
hit on
hit pay dirt
hit the books
hit the bricks
hit the deck
hit the hay
hit the nail on the head
hit the road
hit the sack
hog heaven
hoisted by your own petard
hold the phone
hold your horses
holding all the cards
holy cow
hook me up
hook, line, and sinker
hop, skip, and a jump
hope against hope
hope springs eternal
horny as a toad
horse around
horse of a different color
horse sense
horsing around
hot as hell
hot enough for you
hot enough to fry an egg
hot handed
hot water
house divided
how's it hanging
hump day
hunker down

hurl insults

J

Jack of all trades and a master
of none
jerk off
jiminy Christmas
jockeying for position
joined at the hip
journey of a thousand miles
begins with the first step
jump down your throat
jump in with both feet
jump on the bandwagon
jump the gun
jumped his/her bones
jury is still out
just a cotton pickin' minute here
just a minute
just a second
just around the bend
just fell off the turnip truck
just the tip of the iceberg
justice is blind

K

keep an (my) eye on you
keep it down
keep it simple stupid
keep your fingers crossed
keep your chin up
keep your eyes open
keep your hair on
keep your nose to the
grindstone
keeps his cards close to his
vest
keeps on ticking
kick back

kick him to the curb
kick it
kick some butt
kick the bucket
kick your feet up
kick your heels
kid in a candy store
king's ransom
kiss and tell
kiss ass
kiss my ass
kissing the rose
kit and kaboodle
knee-high to a grasshopper
knife through hot butter
knock it out of the park
knock off
knock on wood
knock your socks off
knocked up
knockout blow
knockout
know it like the back of my
hand
know the ropes
know the score
know what's up
know where you stand
know which side your bread is
buttered on
knows it chapter and verse
knuckle down
knuckle sandwich
knuckle under
Kodak moment

L

land of milk and honey
last ditch effort

last hurrah
last but not least
laugh a minute
laugh all the way to the bank
lay down the law
legend in his own mind
leopard doesn't change its spots
lesser of two evils
let bygones be bygones
let sleeping dogs lie
let the cat out of the bag
let's roll
let's split
lickety-split
licking one's wounds
lie down with lions
life is a bowl of cherries
life's a bitch
light as a feather
light at the end of the tunnel
lights out
like a bull in a china shop
like a chicken with his head cut off
like a coiled spring
like butter
like chalk and cheese
like father like son
like flies on shit
like it's going out of style
like oil and water
like there is no tomorrow
line in the sand
lion's den
lion's share
lipstick on a pig
litmus test
little bird told me

little of this a little of that
live and learn
living high off the hog
lie like a rug
lock, stock, and barrel
long and short of it
long arm of the law
long in the tooth
long row to hoe
long shot
long time no see
long ways away
look before you leap
look into your heart
look out
look over your shoulder
loose cannon
lose your shirt
lose your lunch
loser
lost a step
love is blind
lower than a snake's belly
luck of the draw

M
madder than a wet hen
made it by the skin of my teeth
made of money
mail it in
main dish
make a break for it
make a long story short
make a mountain out of a mole hill
make ends meet
make heads or tails of
make or break
make out like a bandit

make the grade
make tracks
make up
make waves
make your move
man's home is his castle
marked man
marking time
marriage of two minds
matter-of-fact
meet and greet
melting pot
memory like an elephant
mercy me
Mexican standoff
mile high club
milk it for all it's worth
missed the boat
mission critical
Monday morning quarterback
money can't buy happiness
money doesn't grow on trees
money grubbing
money hungry
money is the root of all evil
money makes the world go round
money out the wazoo
monkey business
monkey with
monkey wrench
monkey around
more than meets the eye
more the merrier
more we learn the less we know
mouth off
mud slinging
mug for the camera
Murphy's law

must be seeing things
my bad
my brain is fried
my hands are tied
my stomach is tied up in knots
my way or the highway

N

nail biter
naked as a jaybird
naked as the day you were born
near and dear to my heart
necessary evil
necessity is the mother of invention
nerves of steel
nervous as a cat on a hot tin roof
nervous as a long-tailed cat in a room full of rocking chairs
never put off until tomorrow what you can do today
new lease on life
newbie
nice guys finish last
night and day
nip and tuck
nip it in the bud
no accounting for taste
no brainer
no go
no holds barred
no ifs, ands, or buts about it
no man is an island
no pain, no gain
no shit Sherlock
no skin off my nose
no strings attached

no way José
nod off
none of your business
noodle on
nose in the air
not playing with a full deck
not the brightest bulb
not the brightest crayon
not the ghost of a chance
not the sharpest pencil in the box
nothing personal
nothing to sneeze at
nothing to write home about
nothing up my sleeve
nothing ventured
nothing gained
now or never

Ⓞ

object of desire
off and running
off the cuff
off the hook
off the shelf
off the top of my head
off your rocker
off-kilter
oh brother
oh my goodness
old as dirt
old ball and chain
old school
on a lark
on a roll
on a short leash
on a soap box
on a wing and a prayer
on fire

on par
on pins and needles
on skid row
on tenterhooks
on the back burner
on the ball
on the fly
on the level
on the make
on the road again
on the same page
on the take
on the tip of my tongue
on the up and up
on track
on your toes
once burned twice shy
once in a blue moon
one bad apple spoils the whole bunch
one good turn deserves another
one in million
one man's trash is another man's treasure
one night stand
open book
opportunity knocks
out of gas
out of it
out of pocket
out of sight
out of mind
out of the blue
out of the frying pan and into the fire
out of the woods
out of whack
out to lunch

over a barrel
over and over
over my head
over the hill
over the top

P
pack it in
pain in the butt
pain in the neck
paint yourself into a corner
paper over
paper tiger
par for the course
pass away
pass on
pass the buck
pass the hat
passed with flying colors
path of least resistance
pay as you go
pay lip service
pay the piper
pay through the nose
pearls before swine
peas in a pod
pencil in
penny pincher
penny saved penny earned
penny wise pound foolish
people who live in glass houses
perception becomes reality
phone it in
pick of the litter
picture worth a thousand words
piece of cake
pig-headed
pig out
pin hopes on

piss in the wind
piss-poor
plain and simple
plain as day
plastered
play ball
play by ear
play second fiddle
play the field
play the hand you're dealt
play with the big boys
plunk down
poison the well
poor as a church mouse
pot calling the kettle black
pot of gold at the end of the rainbow
pound for pound
pound of flesh
pound the pavement
preach to the choir
press the flesh
pretty penny
propped up
pull a stunt
pull the wool
pull your leg
pure as the driven snow
push the envelope
push your buttons
push up daisies
put a cork in it
put a lid on it
put a sock in it

Q
quick buck
quiet as a church mouse
quit horsing around

R

rain on my parade
raining cats and dogs
raise the bar
rake in money
rat out
raw end of the deal
read between the lines
read the fine print
read the riot act
real McCoy
red carpet treatment
red herring
reinvent the wheel
rest on your laurels
rhyme or reason
right on the money
right up your alley
ring a bell
roll of the dice
roll out the red carpet
rolling in dough
rolling stone
rollover on
rotten to the core
rough around the edges
rough road
rub salt in the wound
rub your nose in it
rub me the wrong way
run circles around

S

same song and dance
save your breath
say what you will
scared of his own shadow

scrape the bottom of the barrel
second banana
second wind
see eye to eye
see the light
sell out
sensory overload
separate the men from the boys
separate the wheat from the chaff
seven year itch
shit eating grin
shit out of luck
shape up or ship out
sharp as a tack
shed light on
shoestring budget
shoot from the hip
shoot straight
shoot the breeze
shoot yourself in the foot
shop talk
short changed
short fuse
shot in the dark
shotgun wedding
shove off
show the door
show me the money
shut out
shut up
shut your hole
shut your mouth
sick as a dog
sick to death of it
signed, sealed, and delivered
silence is golden

silenced the crowd
sing like a bird
sink or swim
sink your teeth into
sit tight
six of one half a dozen of another
skate on thin ice
skeletons in the closet
slam dunk
slip through your fingers
slippery slope
sloshed
slow as molasses
sly as a fox
small potatoes
small world
smashed
smoke and mirrors
smoking gun
smooth operator
smooth over
SNAFU
snail's pace
snow job
snowball's chance in hell
so close you can taste it
solid as a rock
sound like a broken record
soup to nuts
speak with a forked tongue
spin your wheels
spitting image
split second
splitting hairs
spread the word
spruce up
squeaky wheel
squeal on

stack the deck
state of the art
stay tuned
stem the tide
step on it
step on toes
stick in the mud
stick with it
stiff as a board
stone-faced
stoned
stone's throw away
stop on a dime
stop the presses
straight arrow
stress out
stretch a dollar
string him along
strong as an ox
stubborn as a mule
stick out like a sore thumb
stuck-up
stuffed shirt
suck up
sucker
sugarcoat it
survival of the fittest
swallow one's pride
sweat equity
sweep under the rug
sweet sixteen
sweet deal
sweeten the pot
swim against the tide
swim with sharks

T
tail between his legs
take a back seat

take a breather
take a dump
take a leak
take a step back
take five
take it easy
take it from me
take it to the limit
take it with a grain of salt
take one for the team
take stock of
take the bull by the horns
take the plunge
take the world by storm
take your life in your own hands
taken for a ride
take a toll
talk to the hand
talk shop
talk until you are blue in the face
talking behind his back
tall tale
tanked
taste of your own medicine
teacher's pet
team player
tear you a new hole
tempest in a teapot
ten to one
test the waters
test one's mettle
thank goodness
thank your lucky stars
take the cake
thick-headed
third wheel
thorn in my side

three sheets to the wind
throw a curve ball
throw in the towel
thumbs up
tight wad
tighten your belt
time is money
time on your hands
time out
toy with
toe the line
tongue in cheek
too much information
tooth and nail
top dog
touch and go
toe the line
tried and true
tune out
turn on a dime
turn over a new leaf
twiddle your thumbs
twist my arm
twist of fate
two-faced
two left feet

U

ugly as sin
under a microscope
under her thumb
under the gun
under the knife
until the cows come home
up a creek without a paddle
up for grabs
up in arms
up the ante
uphill battle

V

variety is the spice of life
virgin on prom night

W

wait for the ink to dry
wait for the dust to settle
wait for the other shoe to drop
waiting for your ship to come in
wake-up and smell the coffee
wake-up call
walk on the wild side
walk on eggshells
wash your hands
washed up
wasted
watch the clock
wave a white flag
well off
wet behind the ears
wet blanket
wet dream
what goes around comes around
what goes up must come down
what you see is what you get
whatever floats your boat
whatever tickles your fancy
whatever turns you on
what's up with that

when all is said and done
when hell freezes over
when in Rome
when it rains it pours
where there's smoke there's fire
white elephant gift
white knuckle ride
whole nine yards
wig out
wing it
wipe the slate clean
wishy-washy
worker bee
world of hurt
worm has turned
worry wart
worth its weight
wrong side of the tracks

Y

yank your chain
you ain't seen nothing yet
you can say that again
you snooze you loose
your goose is cooked
you've got nerve

Z

zigged when he should have zagged
zip it
zip your lip

Revision Tips

✎ Turn on the Clichés, Colloquialisms, and Jargon option in the toolbox. They will be marked for you. As you read through your draft, decide which to keep and which to kill. Have you used the cliché intentionally?

✎ Can you twist it or make it fresh?

✎ Have you committed cliché abuse? Should you trim them?

✎ Does the cliché fit the time and place?

✎ Does the cliché fit the background and personality of the character uttering it?

COLLOQUIALISMS, JARGON,

SLANG & PROFANITY

Remember to select "Clichés. Colloquialisms and Jargon" under the Style options (see introduction) and they will be marked for you. This makes them easier to find.

✎ **Colloquialisms** are words or phrases that we use in conversation or informal situations. An example would be the different ways people refer to carbonated beverages: *cola, soda, soda pop,* and *pop*.

Another example is cooked batter: *pancake, griddle cake, flap jack, Johnny cake,* and *short stack*.

They can be words (*gonna*), phrases (*hang on*), or aphorisms (*when the going gets tough, the tough get going*).

A few examples of colloquialisms include:

bat out of hell	crazy as a loon
beating a dead horse	deader than a doornail
bigger than a barn	dumb as stump
bump on a log	drunk as a monkey
couldn't care less	happy as a pig in shit

hell for leather	not the brightest crayon
hotter than hell	older than dirt
knocked into next week	one fry short of a happy meal
like flies on shit	piece of cake
like white on rice	shut your pie hole
meaner than a snake	slow as molasses
neat as a pin	tighter than a banjo string

Colloquialism, clichés, and slang are close cousins and hard to differentiate. In general, colloquialisms are limited to a specific geographic location (the south) and slang is more widespread (America). It isn't important for the sake of revision to worry about the finer points of distinction. We aren't in English class anymore. The important point is to use them wisely.

Both colloquialisms and slang can be used as a dialogue plant and payoff: a phrase repeated two or three times at critical points in the story between two characters. Both can add color to your prose and dialogue. Sprinkled throughout a manuscript, they are fine. A few sprinkled in a paragraph is considered overdoing it.

✐ **Jargon** consists of words that relate to a specific group, profession, or event. It is used as short-hand to refer to things common to people's understanding. If you've ever listened to a professional conversation and been unable to follow the acronyms, you've listened to jargon.

The field of computing has spawned many jargon words: *CD-Rom, disk drive, hard drive, RAM, byte,* and *internet.*

Medicine is full of Latin words that sound intimidating but mean relatively little. Although it is Latin, it is also their jargon. Medical terminology is full of acronyms: CT scan (computed topography), MRI (magnetic resonance imaging), BMP (basic metabolic panel), CBC (complete blood count), and PET scan (positron emission topography).

🖊 **Slang** references words, ideas, knowledge, products, etc. Slang in England is not the same as slang in America.

A few examples of slang include:

A

ace (expert)
a-okay
a-one
air head
all-nighter
all wet
ammo
ante up
armpit (place is an)
awesome

B

bad (meaning good)
barf
bashed
beat (tired)
beemer (BMW)
belly up
bench
bent out of shape
big gun
big mouth
big stink
blade (knife)

blimp (fat)
blow (money, leave, drugs)
blow a fuse
blow one's cool
blown away
bomb (good)
bombed (drunk)
bonkers
boo-boo
boozer
bread (money)
break it up
bring down
bring it up
buck (money)
bum
bummer
bust
buy it

C

call (prediction)
can (toilet)
catch rays
catch Z's

257

cheesy
chicken (coward)
chintzy (cheap)
chow down
clunker
cold fish
collar (catch)
come up for air
con (trick)
cool (good)
cool down
cop (steal)
couch potato
cowboy up
crack open a bottle (open)
cram (study)
cream (beat)
croak (die)
cruise (go fast)
cushy (comfortable)
cut (dilute)
cut out (leave)

D
damage (cost)
dead (boring)
deck (hit)
deep pockets (rich)
dicey (uncertain)
dirty (questionable)
ditch (leave)
do a snow job (lie)
dope (fool or drugs)
dork
dough (money)
down (drink)
drag (bore)
drag queen
dynamite (great)

E
earful (gossip)
easy mark (fool)
eating away (bothering)

F
face-off (oppose)
far-out (good)
fix (dose)
flaky (unreliable)
flick (movie)
flip out
flip side
fox or foxy (pretty)
freebie

G
get into
get it
get with it
gig
glitch
glitzy
go (try)
go bananas
go down (happening)
good vibes
goof
goof up
goofy
gourd (head)
grand (1000)
grass (marijuana)
gravy (easy)
gravy train (rich)
great (meaning not great)
groovy
gross
gross out

grub (food)
grubby
grungy
gut (instinct)

H
hairy (dangerous)
hammer (accelerate)
hammered (drunk)
hang it up (quit)
hang loose (relax)
hang tough
hardware (weapons)
have a buzz (drunk)
have it together (competent)
head honcho (boss)
heave (vomit)
high (on drugs)
history (gone)
hit (success)
hole up (hide)
hooker (prostitute)
hot (good looking)
huffy
hungry (eager)
hustle (hurry)
hyped
hyper

I
I.D. (identification)
in (accepted or popular)
in a jam (in trouble)
in deep (involved)
in the bag (settled)
intense (serious)

J
jam (situation)

jerk
jerk around (waste time)
jock (athlete)
john (toilet or prostitute's customer)
John/Jane Doe (unidentified)
joint (bar or drugs)
junkie (addict)
just off the boat (new)

K
keep cool (calm)
kegger (party)
kick out of (enjoy)
klutz (clumsy)
knock it (insult)
knocked up (pregnant)
knockout (good looking)
knuckle sandwich (punch)
kooks (crazy)

L
laid-back (calm)
lame (inadequate)
line (story)
loser (useless)
love handles (fat)

M
make a move on (seduce)
make waves (cause trouble)
maxed out mean (good)
mega (a lot)
megabucks
mellow (calm)
meltdown
mickey mouse (nonsense)
mush (nonsense)

N

nark (tell on)
neat (good)
negatives (bad things)
nick (steal or arrest)
nip (drink)
no sweat (easy)
nuke (microwave)
nut or nuts (crazy)

O

okay
okie dokie
off your rocker (crazy)

P

pad (apartment)
pain in the neck
paper-pusher
party animal
party hearty
paw (hand)
peanuts (little money)
pickled (drunk)
piece of cake
pig (boorish person)
pig out (eat)
pit stop (bathroom stop)
plastered (drunk)
pooped out (tired or didn't show)
pop (popular or hit)
pop by (visit)
pop for it (pay)
prod (remind)
psyched out
psyched up
psycho
puke (vomit)
push off (go away)

put the move on (flirt)
put-on (fake)

Q

quarterback (lead)
quick buck

R

rack (bed or breasts)
racket (noise)
rag (newspaper or nag)
rap (talk)
rat hole
raw (new)
ream out (yell)
red hot (popular or heated)
repo (a car)
rinky-dink (inferior)
riot (funny)
road hog
rocks (ice or diamonds)
rough time (difficulty)
rug (toupee)
rug-rat (toddler)
run off at the mouth (talk too much)
run out of gas (lose momentum)

S

sack (go to bed or fire someone)
scarf down (eat)
schmuck (jerk)
screw around (waste time)
screw up
sharp (intelligent or attractive)
shoot down (disagree)
shot (try)
slammer (prison)
smashed (drunk)

smoke eater (fireman)
split (leave)
spook (frighten or spy)
spud (potato)
square (old-fashioned)
steamed (angry)
stink (repulsive)
straight (honest)
stressed (upset)
stud (good looking man)
sucker (fool)

T
take a hike (leave)
taken (duped)
taking care of business
threads (clothing)
tool around (drive)
totaled (wrecked)

U
up (happy)
up for grabs

V
veg out (relax)
vibe (feeling)

W
wad (bundle of money)
waste (kill)
wasted (drunk or high)
wheels (car)
whipped (tired)
whiz (smart or talented)
whiz by take a whiz (pee)
wired (alert or on drugs)
wuss or wussy (weak)
wuss out (quit)

Y
yak (talk)
yuk or yukky (bad)
yuk it up (joke)

Z
zip (zero or fast)

✎ **Profanity.** Oh, the hellish question! Dare you use profanity in your writing? It depends on your target audience. Will they be offended? Do you care? Does it fit the context of the plot?

If you are writing about nuns in England in 1300, I doubt they used the F-bomb. You might have a salty old nun who muttered the occasional *"bloody hell"* but only after the reign of Bloody Mary I (queen regent from 1553 to 1558).

Is it appropriate for your target audience? If you write children's picture books or Christian romance, I'd leave it out.

Are you using it to define character? Some characters swear like sailors. Others never would. Do your space aliens have potty mouths? Are your characters living in the ghettos of New York City? If so, drop the F-bomb a few times. Don't use it for shock value. The F-bomb has lost its impact by overuse. It isn't shocking anymore. The F-word is versatile. It is a noun, adjective, and verb, even though it stands for *"For Unlawful Carnal Knowledge"* and did not exist prior to England adopting the acronym. Modern television and film scripts overuse it and it becomes redundant. If it is inserted into every sentence, it feels abusive. No one likes listening to abusive people rant, even in fiction.

A rare profanity inserted for effect is better than twenty in a row. Profanity offends many. They are *red* words and imply anger, even if the person isn't angry. It may limit your audience. It's important to ask how your agent or editor feels about it. If she hates it, she might insist you take it out. If you stand your ground, you may have to find another agent or editor, or publish it yourself.

Revision Tips

✍ Make sure you selected the Cliché, Colloquialism, and Jargon option in the toolkit. The program locates these items for you. You can do a search for a specific set of words. Hit [Control] [F] or Find and Highlight All or Find Next. Save frequently using [Control] [S]. You don't need to search for words you would never use. You can also skim read your printed manuscript and highlight the items as you find them.

✍ Investigate each instance. Is the item necessary? Does it add or detract from what you are trying to say?

✍ Is it used in a new way or twisted into something unique?

✍ Do they serve as emphasis, a splash of color, or is your manuscript drowning in them?

✍ If the same item appears more than once, unless you are using it as a plant or payoff, decide which location you want to keep it in and cut the rest.

✍ Are you using profanity? Do you need to? Should you, given the target audience?

Diana Hurwitz

REDUNDANT WORDS

Redundant words are so common they are hard to recognize. Redundancies use two words when one will do. Search for them all. Choose which ones to keep and which to kill. A character would use redundancies in conversation. Few speak that formally. Cutting some of them feels like amputating a limb. They are found in newspapers, broadcasts, and magazine articles. This rule is broken frequently.

A
absolutely essential
absolutely perfect
absolutely positive
actual fact
advance forward
advance planning
advance preview
advance reservations
advance warning
add an additional
add-up
added bonus
affirmative yes
aid and abet
all-time record

alternative choice
A.M. in the morning
and etc.
anonymous stranger
annual anniversary
armed gunman
artificial prosthesis
ascend up
ask the question
assemble together
attach together
ATM machine
autobiography of his/her own life

B
bald-headed

balsa wood
basic fundamentals
basic necessities
best ever
biography of his–or her–life
blend together
blistering hot
boat marina
bouquet of flowers
brief in duration
brief moment
brief summary
burning embers

C

CD-ROM memory
cacophony of sound
cameo appearance
cancel out
careful scrutiny
cash money
cease and desist
circle around
circulate around
classify into groups
climbed up
close proximity
closed fist
collaborate together
combine together
commute back and forth
compete with each other
completely annihilate
completely destroyed
completely eliminate
completely engulfed
completely filled
completely surround
component parts

confer together
connect together
connect up
confused state
consensus of opinion
constantly maintained
cooperate together
could possibly
crept slowly
crisis situation
curative process
current incumbent
current trend

D

depreciate in value
descend down
desirable benefits
different kinds
disappear from sight
drop down
during the course of
DVD disk
dwindle down

E

each and every
earlier in time
eased slowly
eliminate altogether
emergency situation
empty hole
empty out
empty space
enclosed herein
end result
enter in
entirely eliminate
equal to one another

eradicate completely
estimated at about
evolve over time
exact same
exposed opening
extradite back

F

face mask
fall down
favorable approval
favorite pet peeve
fellow classmates
fellow colleague
few in number
filled to capacity
final conclusion
final end
final outcome
final ultimatum
first and foremost
first conceived
first of all
fly through the air
follow after
foreign imports
former graduate
former veteran
free gift
from whence
frozen ice
frozen tundra
full to capacity
full satisfaction
fuse together
future plans
future recurrence

G

gather together
general public
GOP party
GRE exam
green/blue etc. in color
grow in size

H

had done previously
harmful injuries
head honcho
heat up
HIV virus
hoist up
hollow tube
hurry up

I

illustrated drawing
incredible to believe
indicted on a charge
input into
integrate together
integrate with each other
interdependent on each other
introduced a new
introduced for the first time
ISBN number

J

join together
joint collaboration

K

kneel down
knowledgeable experts

L

lag behind
later time
LCD display
lift up
little baby
live studio
live audience
live witness
local residents
look ahead to the future
look back in retrospect
long-necked giraffe
long-lasting durability

M

made out of
major breakthrough
major feat
manually by hand
may possibly
meet together
meet with each other
mental telepathy
merge together
might possibly
minestrone soup
mix together
modern __of today
mutual cooperation
mutually interdependent
mutual respect for each other
number-one leader in __

N

nape of her neck
native habitat
natural instinct
never before

new beginning
new construction
new innovation
new invention
new recruit
nodded his head
none at all
nostalgia for the past
now pending

O

off of
old adage
old custom
old proverb
open trench
open up
oral conversation
originally created
output out of
outside in the yard
outside of
over exaggerate
over with

P

pair of twins
palm of the hand
passing fad
past experience
past history
past memories
past records
penetrate into
period of time
personal favorite
personal friend
personal opinion
pick and choose

PIN number
pizza pie
plan ahead
plan in advance
plunge down
polar opposites
positive identification
postpone until later
pouring down rain
pre-board an airplane
preheat
pre-record
private industry
present incumbent
present time
previously listed above
proceed ahead
proposed plan
protest against
pursue after

R
raise up
RAM memory
ran quickly
reason is because
reason why
recur again
red color
re-elect for another term
refer back
reflect back
regular routine
repeat again
reply back
retreat back
revert back
rise up
rose to her feet

round in shape

S
safe haven
safe sanctuary
same exact
sand dune
scrutinize in detail
self-___ yourself
sat down
separated apart from each other
serious danger
share together
sharp point
shiny in appearance
shrugged his shoulders
shut down
single unit
sit down
skipped over
slow speed
small leprechaun
small size
small speck
soft in texture
soft to the touch
sole of the foot
spell out in detail
spliced together
stand up
start off
start out
still persists
still remains
stomped heavily
stood to his full height
stood up
sudden impulse
sum total

surrounded on all sides

T
tall in height
tall in stature
temper tantrum
ten in number
terribly bad
the reason why
three a.m. in the morning
three-way love triangle
time period
tiny bit
tiptoed quietly
today's soup du jour
total destruction
true facts
truly sincere
tuna fish
twelve noon
twelve midnight
two equal halves
two-wheeled bicycle

U
ultimate goal

undergraduate student
underground subway
unexpected emergency
unexpected surprise
unintentional mistake
universal panacea
unnamed anonymous
UPC code
usual custom

V
vacillate back and forth
veiled ambush
very pregnant
very unique
visible to the eye

W
wall mural
warn in advance
weather conditions
weather situation
whether or not
white snow
write down

Revision Tips

✍ Do a search using [Control] [F] for redundant words. Eliminate one of the redundant words.

✍ If you keep a redundancy, use it sparingly and for effect.

✍ If you disagree with this rule, ignore it. Make sure your editor and agent feel the same way.

SIMILES, METAPHORS & STUFF

Variety is the spice of life and these rhetorical devices sound like exotic spices. We know how they taste but have forgotten the names. These spices should be sprinkled in carefully. They enrich a sentence or paragraph when you want a little punch. You shouldn't overwhelm the reader with them and should be mindful of clichés. You earn a gold star for using them effectively. You earn two gold stars if you can remember their names.

☆ **Abstraction** advances a proposition from generic to specific.

Jane opened the book[1], a thick tome[2], a collection of poetry[3].

☆ **Alliteration** repeats initial consonants in consecutive or grammatically corresponding words.

Jane opened the diary, the <u>w</u>ild, <u>w</u>ishful, <u>w</u>indow to its owner's soul.

✩ **Amplification** repeats a word or phrase, adding more detail to emphasize a point.

Jane wanted to deny <u>the truth</u>, <u>the truth</u> about the diary[1], <u>the truth</u> about the ghost[2], <u>the truth</u> about herself[3].

✩ **Anadiplosis** repeats a word that ends a phrase, clause, or sentence at the start of the next.

Jane opened a book. The book was a collection of <u>poetry</u>, <u>poetry</u> that made her blush.

✩ **Analogy** compares two things that are alike and is more clinical than a simile. It can use: *also, and so on, and the like, as if,* and *like.*

Jane was drawn to Dick[1] <u>like</u> a humming bird to nectar[2].

✩ **Anaphora** repeats the same word or words at the beginning of each successive clause or sentence. There are at least three or four beats. You can separate the beats with other sentences but they should be in the same paragraph. The last beat should be in the last sentence of the paragraph.

<u>She should</u> have ignored the diary. The truth was too horrible to acknowledge. <u>She should</u> have burned it. <u>She should</u> have escaped while she still had the chance.

★ **Antithesis** connects two contrasting propositions, usually in parallel clauses or sentences.

Jane knew he <u>loved</u> her and she knew he <u>hated</u> her.

★ **Assonance** repeats similar vowel sounds in successive clauses or sentences.

The <u>rain</u> on the <u>plain</u> drove Jane completely <u>insane</u>.

★ **Asyndeton** omits conjunctions and speeds up the sentence using three or four beats.

Dick ran, <u>laughing, hysterical, howling</u> from the library.

★ **Balance** offers two propositions of equal value joined by a comma or semicolon. The second half mirrors the first half but changes a few words.

Dick asked not what Jane could do for him[1], but what he could do for her[2].

★ **Chiasmus** repeats a sentence or clause but reverses the order in the second half.

When the water gets rough, the rough get in the water.

⭐ **Chronicity** moves the sentence backward or forward in time using connectors such as: *after, before, during* and *until.*

<u>Before</u> Dick would agree to enter the library, <u>before</u> he would agree to read the book, he insisted that Jane go home.

⭐ **Conduplicato** repeats a key word from the base clause to start the next sentence or clause.

Dick was <u>hard to</u> love, <u>hard to</u> hate.

⭐ **Consecutive** clauses reveal a series of actions or thoughts.

Dick ran through the hall[1], up the stairs[2], skidding around the corner[3], breaking into the library[4] in time to hear Jane scream.

⭐ **Epanelepsis** repeats the same word or phrase at the beginning and end of a clause or sentence.

<u>Day</u> followed <u>day,</u> <u>week</u> followed <u>week</u>, and Jane still had no answer.

⭐ **Epistrophe** repeats the same word or phrase at the end of successive phrases, clauses, or sentences. It carries emotion.

Jane charmed <u>him</u>, confused <u>him</u>, and consumed <u>him</u>.

✩ **Epizeuxis** repeats a word in a sentence or clause for emphasis.

It was a <u>long, long</u> night for them both.

✩ **Hyperbole** uses deliberate exaggeration. It can be funny or sarcastic. Use it sparingly.

Jane was so tired she could've slept for <u>a year</u>, <u>maybe four</u>.

✩ **Hypophora** is similar to a rhetorical question, only the question is answered. Often the base clause or sentence poses the question and the modifying phrases answer it.

In dialogue, it can be provocative if the character asks the question then answers it for the other person.

Jane turned to Dick. "So you want to slay the ghost, by yourself? No, no, I get it. You're strong; I'm weak. You're fast; I'm slow. I'd just get in your way. Fine, see if I care."

✩ **Isocolon** stresses corresponding words, phrases, or clauses of equal length and similar structure.

Never had Dick promised so much, to appease so many, to benefit so few.

✪ **Litotes** is an understatement that denies the opposite of the word the reader expects. It can use *no* or *not*. It creates confusion.

Jane was <u>not a little angry</u> with Dick for leaving her.

✪ **Metaphors** can add richness and texture if used wisely. Metaphors compare two different things without using *like* or *as* in sentences and paragraphs. Not every simile is a metaphor, but every metaphor implies a simile. Dead metaphors and similes are often cliché, so it's important to cut them or change them up when possible. The biggest offender is the mixed metaphor in which the second proposition is inconsistent with the first.

Dick was able to shed some light on the text.

(light = understanding)

Jane stared through the window at the black velvet sky. (sky = black velvet)

✪ **Oxymorons** connect contradictory terms. You can find extensive lists on the internet. If you look for them, kill them whenever possible. They are hard to spot because they are so frequently used. Most readers won't recognize them as such.

A few examples include:

act naturally	clearly confused	old news
active retirement	controlled chaos	open secret
almost exactly	deafening silence	original copy
approximately equal	exact estimate	seriously funny
blind eye	found missing	unbiased opinion
born dead	larger half	virtual reality

☆ **Parallelism** uses balance and three beats following a sentence or clause with a phrase that starts with a similar kind of word (*adjective, adverb* or *noun*).

The book was <u>damaged</u>[1], <u>damaged</u> beyond all hope of repair[2]. (balance)

Jane loved him more for it[1], <u>more</u> than she loved her books[2], <u>more</u> than she loved herself[3]. (3 beats)

☆ **Personification** attributes an animal or inanimate object with human characteristics.

The <u>book hid</u> its secrets from her.

☆ **Phatics** are used to begin or interrupt the flow of a sentence without adding meaning to it and act as speed bumps. They are used to strengthen the connection to the reader and can impart a confidential tone. It can raise or lower the dramatic potential of a clause, it can emphasize an important claim, certify content, or negate content. Be sure they are not used to preface an information dump.

They include, but are not limited to:

after a fashion
after all
after all is said and done
almost inevitably
amazingly enough
and I agree that it is
and whatnot
as a matter of fact
as everybody knows
as I believe is the case
as is widely known
as it happens
as it turns out
as I've pointed out
as unlikely as it may seem
as we can see
as you can see
at any rate
believe it or not
curiously enough
fittingly enough
for God's sake
for some reason
for that matter
hi
how are you
I am reminded
I can't help but wonder
I might add
I suppose
if conditions are favorable
if I may call it that
if time permits
if truth be known
if you get right down to it
if you know what I mean
if you must know

in a way
in a sense
in my mind
in point of fact
in spite of everything
in the final analysis
it goes without saying
it is important to note
it is important to remember
it occurs to me
it seems to me
it turns out
just between us
just between you and me
let's face it
let me tell you
make no mistake
my Lord
not to mention
of course
one might ask
or as unlikely as it may seem
shall we say
strangely enough
to a certain extent
to be honest
to my dismay
to everyone's surprise
to no one's surprise
to my relief
to my way of thinking
to some extent
what's up
we should remember
when all is said and done
you know
you know what

✰ **Polysyndeton** uses conjunctions to string phrases in a series.

The library was dim and overly warm and full of sneaky shadows.

Neither rain nor snow nor sleet nor hail would keep Dick from finding Jane.

✰ **Polyptoton** repeats words from the same root but with different inflections appear in close proximity.

Dick believed the only thing they had to <u>fear</u> was <u>fearlessness</u>.

✰ **Prefabs** can be used to create two and three beat rhythms to speed the sentence up.

They include, but are not limited to:

boom and bust	hurly-burly	splish-splash
bump and grind	itsy-bitsy	super-duper
daily double	lean and mean	super-saver
doom and gloom	meet and greet	surf and turf
ebb and flow	moldy oldie	teenie-weenie
eager beaver	namby-pamby	thrills and chills
fixer-upper	near and dear	tit for tat
flimflam	oopsy daisy	topsy-turvy
flip-flop	razzle-dazzle	town and gown
harum-scarum	rinky dink	wear and tear
helter-skelter	rise and fall	wheeler-dealer
herky-jerky	rough and ready	whipper-snapper
hip-hop	rough and tough	wild and wooly
hotsy-totsy	rough and tumble	wishy-washy
hour of power	shilly-shally	zigzag

★ **Simile** compares two different things that are similar to each other using *like* and *as*. They often border on cliché. A hidden simile does not use *like* or *as*.

Jane curled up on the couch <u>like</u> a satisfied cat licking her lips.

Jane curled up on the couch, a satisfied cat licking her lips. (hidden)

★ **Symploce** uses anaphora and epistrophe in the same sentence or paragraph. It should appear once or twice in a manuscript for maximum impact and emotion.

Dick should have walked away. He should have put the diary down. He should never have read the shocking words. Jane had charmed him, confused him, and consumed him.

★ **Synecdoche** uses part of something to refer to the whole, a whole thing to refer to a part, a specific thing to refer to a generality, or a generality to refer to a specific thing. It is referring to a *car* as *wheels*, *workers* as *hands*, *eyewear* as *glasses*, and *bandages* as *Band-Aids*.

When it came to books, Jane preferred paper over plastic.

✰ **Tricolon** repeats phrases, clauses, or sentences three times. If the phrases, clauses, or sentences increase in length with each repetition, it is called a tricolon crescendo.

It was a <u>dark</u>, <u>dark</u>, <u>dark</u> moment for them both.

The book was <u>old</u>, <u>old</u> and faded, <u>old</u> enough to be dangerous.

✰ **Zeugma** ends a sentence with a last word or clause that doesn't fit in with the proposition. It offers a twist. It should end a paragraph for maximum effect.

Jane left with her <u>book</u>, her <u>suitcase</u>, and her <u>pride</u>.

Jane <u>needed</u> him and <u>wanted</u> him and <u>wished him dead</u>.

Revision Tips

✍ Look through your work carefully. Highlight each rhetorical device when you find it.

✍ Is the rhetorical device used correctly?

✍ Can it be strengthened?

✍ Is it in the right place for emphasis or placed there accidentally?

✍ Is it formatted correctly?

✍ Is the device overused or cliché abuse?

✍ Does the rhetorical device add to the meaning? Use them for moments when the words really count.

INTERJECTIONS

Interjections are exclamations or parenthetical words that add color to your dialogue or internal dialogue. They express a gamut of emotions: surprise, fear, anger, hate, happiness, joy, glee, disgust, or sarcasm. Make them character specific. Avoid stereotypes. Twist them in new ways.

A
absolutely
abso-freaking-lutely
achoo
ack
adios
adios amigos
adios muchachas
agreed
aha
ahem
ahh
ahoy
alas
all hail
alleluia
aloha
alright
alrighty then
alack

alas
amen
anyhoo
anyhow
anytime
argh
as if
asswipe
attaboy
awww
awful
aye
aye-aye

B
bah
bah humbug
bam
bastard
begorra

behold
bejesus
bingo
bitch
blah
bleck
bleep
bleeping
bless you
blowhard
boo
bravo
brrr
buh bye
bully for you
by god
by cracky

C
cheerio

cheers
ciao
congratulations
cool
crap
creepy
crikey
cripes
crud

D
damn it
dang
dear
darn
drat
duh

E
eek
eew
eh
encore
eureka
excellent

F
fiddlesticks
fie

G
gadzooks
gee
gee whiz
geepers
gesundheit
git
golly
goodbye

good grief
goodness
goodness gracious
gosh
great

H
hah
ha-ha
hallelujah
hardy har har
heigh-ho
hell
hell no
hell yes
hello
hey
hi
hilarious
hmm
ho
ho ho ho
ho hum
hockey sticks
holy buckets
holy cow
holy smokes
hot dog
howdy
hubba hubba
huh
humph
hurray
hush

I
ick
idiot
I'll say

imbecile
indeed
indubitably

J
jackass
jailbait
jeepers creepers
jeez
jerk
Jesus
Jesus, Mary, and
Joseph

K
killjoy
kinky
kiss off
kiss my butt

L
lah-de-dah
liar
lo and behold
loser
louse

M
man
moron
mm-hmm
my bad
my god
my gosh
my word

N
nah
nancy

no

now

now what

nutcase

nut job

O

oh

oh dear

oh my

oh no

oh please

oh well

ole

ooh la la

oomph

oops

ouch

ow

oy

P

pfft

phew

phooey

pip-pip

piss off

piss on it

please

poof

pooh

pow

pshaw

psst

Q

quiet

quit

R

rah rah

rat fink

rats

rat's ass

right

righty-oh

S

sayonara

scat

scoot

scram

sheesh

shh

shit

shoo

shoot

shucks

shush

shut it

shut up

snap

so long

sod off

T

thanks

there

touché

tsk tsk

tut-tut

U

ugh

uh-huh

uh-oh

V

va va va voom

viva

voila

W

wahoo

well

whee

whew

whiner

whoa

whoop

whoop-de-do

whoopee

whoops

whoopsie daisy

woo

woo-hoo

wow

Y

yay

yeah

yes

yikes

yippee

yo

yo ho ho

yoo-hoo

yuck

yuk

yum

yummy

Z

zap

zoinks

zowie

zip it

Revision Tips

✍ Do a search using [Control] [F] or Find for interjections, or read through your printed manuscript and highlight them.

✍ Are they needed?

✍ Are they overused or improperly used?

✍ Have you repeated the same expression too often? Use them sparingly for character definition or plant and payoff dialogue.

ONOMATOPOEIA

We all make sounds. Animals make sounds. It's okay to use sounds once in a while. It's stronger if you use these typical words in a fresh way.

A
achoo
arf
argh

B
baa
babble
bam
bang
bark
bash
bawl
beep
belch
blab
blare
bleat
bleep
blurt
bluster
bobwhite
boing

bong
boo hoo
boom
bop
bowwow
brawl
brring
bubble
bump
burp
buzz
bwahaha

C
cackle
caw
cha-ching
chatter
chime
chirp
chomp
choo-choo
chortle

chuckle
chug
clamor
clang
clank
clap
clash
clatter
click
clip clop
cluck
clump
clunk
cock a doodle doo
coo
cough
crack
crackle
crash
creak
croak
croon

crow
crunch
cry

D
deafening
din
ding dong
drip

E
eew
eek
explode

F
faint
fizz
fizzle
fizzy
flap
flip
flick

flutter

G
gasp
glob
glub
glug
gobble
grate
groan
growl
grr
grumble
grunt
guffaw
gurgle

H
ha ha
hack
harmonious
harumph
hee hee
hee haw
heh
hiss
ho ho ho
honk
hoot
howl
hmph
hum
hush

I
inaudible

J
jangle

jingle

K
kabloowey
keen
kaching
kerplunk
knock knock

M
melodic
meow
mew
mmm
moan
moo
mumble
munch
muahahaha
mumble
murmur
music
mutter

N
neigh
noisy

O
oink
oomph
oompah
ooze

P
patter
peal
peep
pfft

phooey
ping
pong
patter
pitter
plink
plonk
plop
pop
pow
purr
putt

Q
quack
quiet

R
racket
rasp
rat-a-tat
rattle
rawr
ribbit
ring
rip
roar
rumble
rustle

S
screech
scream
shuffle
sh
shush
sigh
sizzle
skitter

slam
slam-bang
slap
slash
slosh
slither
slurp
smack
smash
snap
snarl
sneeze
snore
snort
snuffle
sob
splat
splatter
splish
splash
splosh
splutter
squawk
squeak
squeal
squelch
sss
stamp
stomp
swish
swoop

T
tap
thud
thump
thunder
thwack
tick tock

ting	**U**	whisper	yell
tinkle	ugh	whirr	yelp
toll	uh oh	whistle	youch
tom tom	umph	whine	yuk
toot		whizz	
trickle	**W**	whoop	**Z**
trill	waffle	whoosh	zap
trumpet	wallop	woo	zip
tuwhit	whack	woot	zoom
tuwhoo	wheeze	woof	zzz
twang	whew		
tweet	whimper	**Y**	
twitter	whinny	yawn	
	whip	yiff	

Revision Tips

✎ Do a search using [Control] [F] or Find, or read through your manuscript and highlight the words. Have you used each word more than a few times?

✎ Can you change it up? Can you use the word in an unusual way?

✎ Is the sound necessary? Does it add something to the sentence? If not, cut it.

SENTENCE STRUCTURE

The term *sentence structure* invokes horrible flashbacks to high school and diagramming sentences. Unless you pursued a degree in English, you have probably forgotten how. We will touch on the basics then reveal the magic of using cumulative sentences. Crafting them is an expert level tool.

Examining your manuscript at the sentence and paragraph level may not interest you. You may think it is too fussy or too time consuming. If you choose to do so, you can elevate your work from bland to brilliant.

Unless you had the benefit of a Masters in Fine Arts program, you may be unaware of the full toolbox sentences offer. Learning complex structure not only makes you a better writer, it makes you a more appreciative reader. You will understand the richness and artistry of the prose you admire.

Most writers have read that they are supposed to vary sentence structure to keep their prose from being boring. We will explore when and how to do so.

By controlling the length of your sentences, you control the rhythm. As in poetry, long beats mixed with short beats are satisfying. The heart beats four times as the valves open and close: *thump, Thump, thump, Thump*. We are also attracted to things that come in threes.

Short, long, short, long: Jane sat. She lifted the teacup to her lips. She paused. The steam warmed her cheeks.

Short, long, long: Jane sat. She lifted the teacup, allowing the steam to warm her cheeks.

Short, long, long, long: Jane sat. She lifted the teacup, pausing halfway to her lips, allowing the steam to warm her face.

Long, short, long: Jane lifted the teacup, allowing the steam to warm her cheeks. She sipped. The brew tasted bitter and slightly floral.

Long, long, short: Jane lifted the teacup, allowing the steam to warm her cheeks. It smelled slightly floral and nauseating. She sipped.

You can mix and match sentence lengths for maximum effect once you understand them.

▭ Basic Sentence or Clause

A basic sentence is considered one beat. It offers one proposition. A single beat can be powerful. It adds emphasis to a paragraph and is used sparingly and for impact. If every sentence were basic, you'd sound like you were writing for kindergarteners. We can't have that, unless you are writing a children's picture book.

A basic sentence has a subject and verb.

Sally ran.

Dick laughed.

Jane wept.

The noun may have a modifier.

Pretty Sally ran.

Depressed Jane wept.

The verb may have a modifier.

Sally ran fast.

Sally ran really fast.

The verb may have an object.

Sally threw the ball.

Spot chased the stick.

⌨ Compound Sentence

A compound sentence has two or three equal beats and is the workhorse of sentences. It is used frequently and is a moderate pace. It can advance, refute, or modify one proposition. It can offer two or more propositions. It gives some detail but not too much. The propositions are equal and can be joined with a coordinating conjunction, comma, or semicolon.

A sentence can contain two propositions.

Dick ran and Sally laughed.

Dick laughed as Jane wept.

Spot barked and Puff meowed.

The nouns can have modifiers.

Silly Dick laughed as pretty Jane wept.

The verbs may have modifiers.

Dick laughed softly and Jane wept loudly.

The verbs may have objects.

Dick threw the ball, but Spot chased the cat.

One proposition can be expanded.

Dick kicked the ball, but it fell short of the goal.

Sally wept because Jane fell down.

Three propositions can be offered.

Dick ran, caught the bus, and made it to work on time.

⌨ Sentence Fragments

A sentence that fails to stand alone, lacking either subject or verb, is a sentence fragment. A sentence fragment may locate something in time and place with a phrase or series of phrases, but it lacks proper subject-verb relationship within an independent clause.

In September, before school started, and vacation ended.

The sentence contains three nouns: *September, school,* and *vacation.* It contains two verbs: *started* and *ended.* However, there is no subject performing the action of a verb because you prefaced the subject and verbs with *before.* You repair the fragment by adding the missing subject or verb.

In September, school started and vacation ended.

A sentence fragment can contain a verb phrase that wants to modify something, but the subject is lacking.

Running hard and fast in an attempt to catch up.

There is a verb, *running*, but not a subject. To fix this fragment you need to add a subject.

Dick ran hard and fast to catch up.

Running hard and fast, Dick attempted to catch up.

Dick attempted to catch up by running hard and fast.

The fragment may be missing an actual verb for the subject to perform.

Some of the kids studying in Dick's class last year.

Some of the kids did what? They studied, but that is not the verb for the subject. An *ing* verb form without an auxiliary form is not a verb. You can fix this fragment by adding an action.

Some of the kids studying in Dick's class last year won prizes.

A sentence fragment may have a subject and verb, but they have been subordinated by a dependent word and cannot stand by themselves.

Even though Dick was the better player and by far the most entertaining.

Dick was entertaining and a better player. However, that is not the subject and verb relationship needed. You fix the fragment by removing *even though* or adding a clause to finish the thought.

Dick was the better player and by far the most entertaining.

Even though Dick was the better player, and by far the most entertaining, he didn't make the team.

There are occasions when a sentence fragment can be stylistically effective. It says exactly what you want and no more. Sentence fragments can be used intentionally for impact.

Dick said he was willing to do whatever it took. No matter what.

Make sure you use fragments for a valid reason and that you use them sparingly. A fragment can speed up the text or slow it down, depending on placement and context. It can balance a cumulative sentence. A few times in a manuscript is fine. A few times on a page is not. If you have the toolkit turned on, it identifies sentence fragments for you.

▭ Run-ons

Run-ons are separate sentences that are joined by commas instead of separated by periods. Unintended run-ons should be fixed. If you are in an action sequence or fight scene, you might throw in a cumulative sentence, but not a run-on. A cumulative sentence is intentional and effective. A run-on sentence is not. The way to identify the run-on is to consider how many concepts you are presenting in one sentence. If it reads like a laundry list, it is probably a run-on.

Sally turned off the alarm, tossing on her clothes as she gulped down coffee and drove to the office, barely sliding through security at five past eight.

This is a run-on sentence. To fix it you would chop it up.

Sally turned off the alarm and tossed on her clothes. She gulped down coffee as she drove to the office. She slid through security at five past eight.

Kill all run-on sentences. You may replace a few with artfully crafted cumulative sentences.

▭ Cumulative or Complex Sentences

Cumulative sentences are high art and employ the delicious rhetorical devices we explored earlier. A brilliantly worded cumulative sentence can advance you from rookie to expert.

A complex sentence has multiple beats. It contains the main proposition or clause and is expanded, refuted, or supported by at least two independent clauses and one or more subordinate clauses. Cumulative sentences slow down the pace. They demand attention. Cumulative sentences force your verbal camera to pan, circle, twist, build suspense, zoom in, zoom out, pause, expand, and contract.

Too many cumulative sentences in a row are tedious. Use them sparingly for specific effect.

To clarify and refine the base proposition, adding detail and suspense:

The candle burned brightly, casting shadows on the open book, obscuring the words on the page, forcing Jane closer.

The book lay open, the scrawled handwriting beckoning, the words running together, in haste or in fear.

Zoom from general to specific detail:

The library was unlocked, the interior dim, the book waiting, accusing, pages frail and browning, the words running together.

The moor spread out, treacherous and beautiful, splotches of purple and gray, the peat a trap waiting to swallow her.

Pan away from the point of interest:

Jane walked slowly, her boots treading mud, the road veering sharply, the sky threatening rain.

Jane fingered the blossom, its petals swaying in the breeze, the trees swishing overhead like fans, the sky a turbulent blue.

Deliver the most important proposition last, drawing out the suspense:

Jane walked slowly, her boots treading mud, the road veering sharply, the knife in her hand.

Jane fingered the blossom, pale and lovely, its stem easily cut, its poison invisible.

Separate the base clause, delaying the verb: this tactic risks alienating the reader or creating confusion.

Jane, fey and fickle, fragile and funny, rushed into the garden.

Sally, wise and wonderful, sneaky and snarky, joined the conversation.

Delay the base clause with modifying phrases beginning with *although, even, if, even when, even while*:

If Jane hid, patiently tending the garden, deadheading the flowers, ignoring the shadows on the sundial, Dick would confront the ghost alone.

Though she was the one who found the book, though she was the one who deciphered the text, Dick decided to face the ghost without her.

Delay the base clause by extending the subject:

To be trapped on the moor, in this castle, in this room, frightened her.

If she hadn't opened the book, if she hadn't read the text, if she hadn't reached a conclusion her mind accepted but her heart could not, Jane would have fled.

Delay by interrupting the base proposition by a colon or semicolon, with modifying phrases that support, refute, or extend the base proposition:

The truth about ghosts is that they select you; they scan the thrumming crowd in search of a mind that is open to receive them.

Reverse time and switch focus:

Jane walked slowly, her boots treading mud, the road veering sharply, drawing her toward the mist-shrouded castle.

Jane fingered the blossom, pale and lovely, fluttering in the brisk breeze, it's fragrance a reminder of the love she lost.

Highlight the base clause:

They sat, Jane silently, unwilling to break the silence, Dick forcefully, stirring the papers on the table.

Jane and Dick entered the library, Jane reluctantly, Dick eager to begin.

To further refine each phrase:

The library was ransacked, the books scattered, their pages unbound, the pages holding the secrets she needed to uncover.

To set up a base clause for maximum impact:

Jane could have walked out the door, down the steps, through the breezeway, into the stables and mounted a horse. She could have broken free, free from the castle, the treacherous moor, and the weight of expectation. She stayed.

Revision Tips

✍ Examine your manuscript. Draw lines between the paragraphs.

✍ Decide where the tempo needs to change and mark each section S for slow, M for medium, F for fast, and H for high speed. Take a look at your paragraphs and the content. What are they doing? What should they be doing?

✍ Are they speeding up where you need speed, slowing down when you need to slow down?

✍ Look at sentence length. Circle really short sentences. Underline really long sentences. Are they structured correctly and are they serving the appropriate function?

✍ Make sure you are not "*bad*" telling.

Diana Hurwitz

LEVEL THREE: PROOFREADING

Proofreading is one of the most time consuming and irritating parts of revision. Hunting down rogue periods and spaces should be done with frequent breaks. It has been known to induce catatonia.

You must do this with [Reveal Codes] ¶ on.

You should do this multiple times with the electronic version and at least twice with the printed version. Have someone else help you if they are willing. Once you have a final manuscript, or printed proof in your hands, go over it again, and again, and again.

Your readers will thank you for it.

CAPITALIZATION

The basic rules of capitalization are fairly simple, but there are exceptions to every rule. When to capitalize trips up the best of writers.

✏ Abbreviations

Not all abbreviations are capitalized. When it doubt, look them up. The internet is your friend.

Washington D.C. is capitalized. The abbreviations *i.e.* and *e.g.* are not unless they appear, for some bizarre reason, at the beginning of a sentence.

✏ Acronyms

The letters of an acronym should all be capitalized without periods separating them. There may be a few artistic variances, but they are rare and are typically part of a logo.

ABC	CIA	NHL	VHF
NBC	USA	TV	ADA
CBS	BBC	USB	RNA
FBI	NBA	UHF	DNA

✐ Directions

Capitalize *East, North, Northeast, Northwest, South, Southeast, Southwest,* and *West* when they refer to specific regions.

The Civil War pitted the North against the South

Central America bridges North America and South America.

You do not capitalize directions when referred to generically.

We are heading south for the winter.

✐ Artwork and Media

Capitalize the first and last words of all article titles, book titles, magazines, newspapers, paintings, radio stations, sculptures, and television stations.

United Artists Cinemas

The New York Times

Capitalize other words within the titles such as *is, are,* and *be.*

Do not capitalize these words within titles: *a, an, as, but, if, nor, or,* and other prepositions regardless of their length.

The Wind and The Willows.

The Adventures of Alice in Oz.

How to Sell a Million Books in Five Days.

Capitalize the first letters of legal and government documents.

The Bill of Rights

The Declaration of Independence

Article XIII, Section V, Paragraph III

✎ **Bureaus, Clubs, Committees, Departments, and Groups**

Capitalize the first letters of county, corporate, federal, government, state, and university committees and departments when referred to as proper nouns.

the Department of Defense

our Armed Forces

the United States Air Force

Army, Navy, and Marines

Joint Chiefs of Staff

the Supreme Court

the English Department.

Capitalize the first letters of groups.

Boy Scouts

Girl Scouts

Green Berets

Salvation Army

Red Cross

Navy Seals

Task Force One

Do not capitalize them if you are referring to them generically.

Dick is a real boy scout.

We will set up a task force to handle it.

Capitalize the words federal and state when used as part of an official agency name.

The Federal Bureau of Investigation is hiring translators.

The State Health Board states otherwise.

The State has entered evidence.

Do not capitalize them when used generically.

Don't make a federal offense out of it.

How many states have you visited?

We need to report local, state, and federal income tax.

🖉 Business Names

Capitalize the first letter of all business names when referring to them as proper nouns.

Company

Corporation

Incorporated

Inc.

LLC

Western Union

Pepsi Cola

Procter & Gamble

Do not capitalize company and corporation when referring to them generically.

We went to the company picnic.

We will form a corporation.

✐ Dates and Days of the Week

Capitalize all months and days of the week.

Days: Monday, Tuesday, Wednesday, Thursday, Friday, Saturday, Sunday.

Months: January, February, March, April, May, June, July, August, September, October, November, December.

Do not capitalize seasons unless they are part of a title.

Seasons: spring, summer, winter, fall.

✐ Ethnicities

Capitalize ethnicities such as *Asian, African, Indian,* and *Polynesian.*

✐ Geography and Buildings

Capitalize the first letter of the following items when referring to them as proper nouns.

alleys	drives	peaks	sculptures
attractions	forts	ponds	sports
buildings	historic sites	providences	fields
capitols	houses...	provinces	stadiums
castles	(if named)	roads	statues
cities	lakes	railways	streets
colleges	lanes	rivers	theaters
continents	mountains	roads	towns
counties	monuments	seas	townships
countries	museums	shires	universities
creeks	oceans	states	

Mount Etna

The Eiffel Tower

Lake Tahoe

The Pacific Ocean

Do not capitalize them when referring to them generically.

Dick entered the alley.

Jane photographed the monuments in the park.

Sally loves the ocean.

✐ Honorary Titles, Degrees and School Subjects

Capitalize a person's title when it comes before the name.

Admiral	Judge	Prince
Chairman	His Highness	Princess
Chief	Lady	Professor
Chief Inspector	Lieutenant	Queen
Count	Lord	Representative
Countess	Marquis	Secretary
Deputy	Marquess	Senator
Deputy Chief	Mayor	The Right
Inspector	Mr.	Honorable
Doctor	Mrs.	Vice-Count
Duchess	Miss	Vice-Countess
Duke	Nurse	Vice-President
Earl	Officer	Your Highness
General	President	
Governor	Prime Minister	

Do not capitalize the word if it is being referred to generically.

All the senators and representatives are in session.

Dick will become president of the Kiwanis club next year.

He is a prince among men.

I'll ask high highness if he'd like a beer.

Capitalize a title if used generically as an address.

"How much is this going to cost me, Doctor?"

"What did you say, Chairman?"

You should capitalize honorary titles that come after the name.

Assistant Manager	CPA
Associate	Certified Public Accountant
Attorney at Law	Esquire
CEO	Manager
Chief Executive Officer	President
CFO	Vice President
Chief Financial Officer	

Don't capitalize honorary titles when referred to generically.

We're looking for a general manager.

Dick needs a good attorney.

You should capitalize college degrees and their acronyms when referenced specifically.

Doctor of Veterinary Medicine

Masters in Business Administration

Masters in Finance

Masters in Science

PhD

Dick earned a Masters in Finance. (note the "in" is not capitalized)

You should always capitalize words denoting school subjects that are derived from proper nouns.

The school will offer Chinese, English, French, German, Italian, Japanese, Latin, and Spanish this year.

Sally is taking English next quarter.

You should capitalize school subjects when they are referred to formally.

Sally's degree required her to take: Biology, Geography, Geometry, Health, History, Language Arts, Journalism, Math, Philosophy,

Physics, Physical Science, Psychology, and Social Science.

Jane is taking History and Physics this quarter.

Next semester, Dick must take Physics III, Calculus I, and English 301.

Do not capitalize school subjects when referred to generically.

Dick's degree has strenuous math and science requirements.

✐ Proper Names

Capitalize the first letter of proper names (first, last, and middle names) unless they are being used for a different purpose.

Dick signaled for the bill.

Jane will sally forth.

✐ Salutations and Complimentary Closes

Capitalize the first word of a salutation.

Best Regards	Love	Truly
Dear	Sincerely	Yours Very Truly
My Dear	To Whom It May	Yours
My Dearest	Concern	

✎ Sentences

Capitalize the first word in a sentence and the first word appearing after a period, question mark, or exclamation point.

Jane wanted a cookie, or did she? Dick wanted a cookie

Jane shouted, "Yes!" She hugged Dick.

Do not capitalize dialogue tags *said, asked, etc.*

Do not capitalize the *he* and *she* before a dialogue tag.

"I don't want to," she said.

Do not capitalize the first word appearing after a colon or semicolon unless two or more sentences follow a sentence ending with a colon.

Jane had so many things to do: editing, proofreading, and formatting.

I love Jane's poetry: Her anthology, *A Million Miles*, was heartbreakingly lovely. Her second anthology, *The Road Not Taken*, will be released next month.

Revision Tips:

✍ If you have the toolkit turned on, capitalization errors should be highlighted. That does not eliminate the need to proofread for capitalization.

✍ When proofreading a print copy, highlight words you are unsure of and look them up.

✍ When proofreading a print copy, make sure you have not forgotten to capitalize after a period, etc.

✍ When proofreading dialogue, make sure *he* and *she* before a dialogue tag are not capitalized.

PLURALS

Plurals can be confusing. It's difficult to memorize every instance, but general rules apply. When in doubt, look it up.

Plurals can be checked as you go through other editing passes such as punctuation. If you have the toolkit turned on, the most obvious infractions will be highlighted. Unfortunately, it won't help you with all of them. You must examine your manuscript to catch the less obvious errors.

✎ **Abbreviations, acronyms, numbers, and words as** *words*

An apostrophe is used to make a plural if you are referring to a number or letter of the alphabet.

Computer language is made up of 1's and 0's.

The game consists of a series of X's and O's.

Jane's grades were all A's and B's.

319

Do not use apostrophes to make plurals of acronyms unless the acronym ends in S.

ABCs IRAs URLs MRIs SOS's ROS's

Abbreviations can have plural forms and not all are written in ALL CAPS.

dpi (dots per inch)

mpg (miles per gallon)

rpm (rotations per minute)

psi (pressure per square inch).

Since the first letter stands for a plural, you do not need to add an *s* at the end to make it plural. It is 600 *dpi*, not *dpis*. It is 60 *mpg*, not *mpgs*. It is often written that way, but is technically incorrect. There are exceptions to every rule.

RBI (runs batted in) is referred to as RBIs when talking about baseball stats.

MRE (meals ready to eat) is referred to as MREs.

POW (prisoners of war) is referred to as POWs.

Some errors have been misused so often, they are considered correct.

An apostrophe is not used to make a plural when referring to a word as a word, but the word is italicized.

I found twenty *buts* in that chapter.

The run-on sentence contained six *ands*.

An apostrophe is not used to create the plural of a word.

I learned the ins and outs of publishing the hard way.

His answers were all yeses and nos.

The team had four outs in the last inning.

Do not use an apostrophe to create a plural when referring to an era, form number, or other abbreviation.

America was colonized in the 1400s.

I haven't received my W2s.

There are several methods for measuring IQs.

✐ **Singular nouns**: Most nouns are made plural simply by adding an **s**: *pies, cakes, muffins, drinks,* and *states.*

Nouns that end in *ch, x, s,* or *s*-sounds require *es*: *matches, sexes, classes, buses,* and *busses.*

Nouns with irregular plural forms include: *children, deer, geese, men, mice, people,* and *women.*

Nouns that are Latin or Greek maintain their native plural forms: *alumni, appendices, bases (pl. basis), cacti, crises, criteria, foci, fungi, indices, syllabi,* and *theses (pl. thesis).*

Nouns that end in a consonant plus *y* are made plural by changing the *y* to an *i* and adding *es*. This rule does not apply to proper nouns such as *the Kennedys*.

baby → babies

mommy → mommies

mummy → mummies

gallery → galleries

There are exceptions:

galley → galleys

Nouns that end in *o* get an *s* or *es*. When in doubt, look them up.

hero → heroes

zero → zeroes

potato → potatoes

tomato → tomatoes

Oreo → Oreos

Jello → Jellos

hello → hellos

radio → radios

stereo → stereos

Nouns that end in *f* or *fe* usually change the *f* to a *v* and add *s* or *es*, but there are exceptions. When in doubt, look them up.

calf → calves

elf → elves

half → halves

hoof → hooves

knife → knives

leaf → leaves

life → lives

wife → wives

self → selves

shelf → shelves

wharf → wharfs → wharves

belief → beliefs

chief → chiefs

dwarf → dwarfs

proof → proofs

roof → roofs

waif → waifs

Nouns that appear to be plural can take a singular verb.

The news is good.

Mathematics is fun to learn.

Economics is boring.

There are nouns that appear to be singular but take on a plural form and require a plural verb: *glasses, panties, pants,* and *scissors.* To test this, add on the phrase *a pair of* before the word.

When nouns are used as titles or refer to a word as a word, it is singular and requires a singular verb.

Faces was the name of the Rod Stewart's group.

Postcards from the Edge is Jane's favorite movie.

The Brothers Karamazov is a fun read.

Compound words are complicated. When in doubt, look them up.

mothers-in-law (not mother-in-laws)

There was a room full of mediums that the media attacked.

Dick is an alumni. Jane is an alumnae. Both are alumnus of the university.

Note: both men and women are often referred to as *alumni* these days or *alumnis* which is incorrect. *Alumnus* is the plural.

It used to be *actors* and actresses, but some sources now use actor for both male and female performers.

Nouns that follow the phrase *one of the* are always plural.

one of the boys

one of the girls

one of the reasons

one of the points

When you are speaking of *a number of things*, it is singular.

The number of things Dick does for Jane is astronomical.

When you are using the word number to mean group, it is plural.

A number of editors might agree.

✒ **Family names**: Proper nouns that are family names are pluralized by adding an *s*, unless they end in *ch*, *s*, *sh*, *x*, or *z*, in which case, you add *es*.

Jane invited the Bakers, Hortons, Smiths, and Wilsons.

Dick added the Chavezes, Charleses, Jonses, Maddoxes, Marches, and Williamses.

Proper family names are not pluralized by an *'s*. The apostrophe indicates possession.

Jane visited the Bakers' house, the Hortons' house, and the Smiths' house.

Dick visited the Chavezes' house, the Jonses' house, and the Maddoxes' house.

Proper family names that end in *s* with a hard *z* sound do not have an *s* or *es* added to make them plural.

The Ropers (not *Roperses*) are coming for dinner.

The Rogers (not *Rogerses*) used to live across the street.

The Stephens (Not *Stephenses*) are going on vacation.

✎ **Numbers**: Numerical expressions are mostly singular, but can be plural if the individual parts are acting alone.

Five thousand dollars would sway me.

Half of the faculty is on vacation.

Most of the students have jobs.

✒ **Subjects and predicates, singular versus plural.**

When the noun is singular and the predicate (the phrase that modifies the nouns) is plural, it is some times easier to rework the sentence than figure it out. Even expert writers make mistakes.

My favorite <u>breakfast</u> <u>is</u> pancakes, sausage, eggs, and tea.

This sentence could be modified to read:

My favorite breakfast consists of pancakes, sausage, eggs, and tea.

Turned around the sentence would read:

Pancakes, sausage, eggs, and tea are my favorite breakfast.

A plural subject can be linked to singular predicate.

<u>Mistakes</u> in the manuscript <u>are</u> the problem.

The <u>problem</u> <u>is</u> mistakes in the manuscript.

In these instances, the subject, not the predicate, is singular and determines the verb. A subject may not seem to relate to its predicate.

Incorrect: All students must report to their homeroom teachers. (each homeroom has one teacher)

Correct: All students must report to their homeroom teacher.

Incorrect: All boys want to be like their fathers. (a boy has one father).

Correct: All boys want to be like their father.

Nouns are treated as singular if they represent something people own in common.

Our family is big.

Nouns are treated as singular if they are figurative.

All of us are guilty of having a sweet tooth.

Everyone has teeth. More than one person would certainly have more than one tooth, but the word sweet tooth is figurative. Another awkward example:

Incorrect: We all needed pillows for our beds.

Correct: We all needed pillows for our bed.

We all need pillows. We all have a head. We only need pillows for one bed at a time. The correct version sounds like they are sharing a bed. Reword it and move on.

The audience jumped to their feet.

Why? Because they have two feet each.

Incorrect: Sally, Dick, and Jane need to move their cars.

Correct: Sally, Dick, and Jane need to move their car.

Why? They have one car each. A person could have more than one car, though. To avoid these speed bumps, reword them. If you are tripping over the sentence, your reader will too.

I needed a pillow for my bed.

You need to move your car.

Revision Tips

✍ Underline or highlight singular noun/plural predicate and plural noun/singular predicate combinations. Are they presented correctly?

✍ Do the subject and verb agree?

✍ Does the sentence need to be reworded for clarity?

✍ Do the noun and pronoun agree?

PUNCTUATION

Punctuation marks serve as traffic signs. They pause, connect, and end sentences. Without punctuation, you would have endless blocks of letters all jammed together. You need spaces, quotation marks, commas, hyphens, colons, and semi colons. Using them properly is essential, though most of us forgot how after high school.

To make sure you have the correct punctuation, you should review the draft at microscopic level with [Reveal Codes] ¶ turned on. Setting [View] at [Page Width] prevents your eyes from crossing. I recommend doing this pass at the end, separate from the other passes. It's too easy to get caught up in changing things and skip over this essential step. If you revise heavily as you go, you'll have to do it all over again anyway. This step makes you irritable. Keep the caffeine or your beverage of choice close at hand.

✐ Apostrophes

An apostrophe indicates that a word is either a contraction or a possessive. Contractions include *can't, won't,* and *don't.* Make sure the apostrophe comes before the *t* (don't) instead of after it (*dont'*) or is not in the wrong place (*should'nt, do'nt*). The apostrophe makes up for the missing letters, such as the *o* in not.

An apostrophe indicates ownership of a thing. To create most possessives you add *'s* to the noun or proper noun.

Dick's dog is Spot.

Sally's jump rope broke.

At year's end, we'll all go on vacation.

Exceptions come with pronouns: *his, hers, theirs, its, my, ours,* and *yours.*

What happens when the singular noun or proper noun ends in *s*? The rules state that you should still add the *'s*. Some style guides and editors say there is no need for the second *s*. Some argue that you should drop the extra *s* only on words of several syllables, but retain it on short words. Choose one method and make it consistent.

All of these examples would be considered correct:

The Jones' dog sat.

The Jones's dog sat.

Marlis' clothes are new.

Marlis's clothes are new.

Arkansas' senate is in session.

Arkansas's senate is in session.

Another rule dictates whether a plural noun ending in *s* should have an apostrophe only or *'s*. In this instance, you put the apostrophe after the *s*.

The Smiths' uncut grass is annoying.

The schools' buses all park in the same lot over the summer.

The classes' grades are posted.

The apostrophe is never used to make nouns plurals. It is used to make letters and numerals plural.

Dick got all A's and B's on his report card.

Dick had two 100's and three 50's resulting in a combined score of 350.

✏ Brackets

Brackets can be used to include explanatory words or phrases within quotes.

Dick Doe, the professional sleuth, said that Chief Inspector Barnaby [of Midsommer CID] was an asset to his unit.

Brackets can be used to insert information into a quote.

Dick alleges the defendant falsified [his] tax returns.

Brackets can be used with ellipsis to set off language omitted from a quotation.

Dick alleged the defendant [...] also falsified his tax returns.

Brackets are used with [sic] to indicate misspelled or inappropriately used words within quotations.

Sally found three mispelings [sic] in the manuscript.

Use it only when it is important to maintain the original spelling for some reason. If you can remove the error without violating ethical or professional standards, do so instead. Sic means *thus* or *that is how it was*. It is not an abbreviation and does not require a period.

Use brackets if you italicized or underlined words within quoted language that were not italicized or underlined in the original.

It was the *hush* in the courtroom that made Dick nervous, not the eight jurors [italics added].

Use brackets to include parenthetical phrases inside parenthetical material.

Jane was Chairman of the Kiwanis Club (a thankless position [unpaid]) for ten years.

Use brackets sparingly and only if essential.

✎ Colons

The colon is relatively simple, but extremely effective. A colon is a warning sign. It signals the reader that something really important is ahead, so they better listen. What follows the colon should be important, relevant, and deserve the volume.

A colon is also used to warn that a list will follow. Lists are boring. Use them only if you absolutely have to.

Jane purchased the following: curtains, bedding, towels, and rugs.

A colon can introduce a word to give it punch. This should be limited to two or three times in an entire manuscript.

Dick had only one thing in mind: murder.

A colon can introduce a phrase. This should be limited to two or three times in an entire manuscript for effect.

Dick cased the mall with one objective: to find the thief.

A colon can introduce another sentence. This should be limited to two or three times in an entire manuscript for effect. This is not the way to create suspense.

Dick had one objective: he had to find Sally.

To determine if you need a colon, read the sentence. When you reach the colon, substitute the word *namely*. If the sentence reads smoothly, you need a colon. If it sounds off, you don't.

Dick had one objective, namely he had to find Sally.

Dick had one thing in mind, namely murder.

This test may not work one-hundred percent of the time, but it is a fairly reliable indicator of whether you need a colon.

Do not place a colon after the verb in a sentence, even when you are introducing something, because the colon would be redundant.

Incorrect: Dick's favorite foods are: steak, potatoes, and corn.

Correct: Dick's favorite foods are steak, potatoes, and corn.

If you used the above test, the sentence would read:

Dick's favorite foods are namely steak, potatoes, and corn.

The colon halts the sentence. Make sure you want your reader to stop at that point and really listen to what you say next.

✏ Commas

Commas are the bane of my existence. I think I have a good grasp on them with every daft. I'm wrong. It doesn't matter how many times I edit; I have to do a final comma search on every manuscript. Even then, I could probably be tarred and feathered for the ones that I miss.

Commas force a reader to slow down for a second. Compound sentences, most modifying clauses, and many phrases require commas. There are four main times to use a comma:

Commas separate items in a series. In previous eras, you were required to insert a comma before the final item in a series. It is called the Oxford comma. Some editors say the comma isn't necessary and they are annoyed by them. Other grammar sticklers are annoyed that you didn't use it.

If you have extremely long, complex lists, it is best to use the extra comma. Omit the comma if your sentence is short (five to ten words). Readers can easily follow a short sentence.

With: Sally's bouquet had yellow roses, pink carnations, white baby's breath, and green ferns.

Without: Sally's bouquet had yellow roses, pink carnations, white baby's breath and green ferns.

With: Jane used her lottery money to buy a car, a house, and a Mercedes.

Without: Jane used her lottery money to buy a car, a house and a Mercedes.

With: Jane needed to rent a car, and she needed one fast.

Without: Jane needed to rent a car and she needed one fast.

Some would argue this comma is unnecessary because the sentences are short:

Sally is young, and she is pretty.

Sally is young and she is pretty.

Of course, the sentence could be tightened further:

Sally is young and pretty.

Choose which method works for you, or satisfies your editor, and keep it consistent.

Mistakenly leaving commas out can affect the meaning of your sentence.

Without: The panda bear eats bamboo shoots and leaves *(meaning he eats both a bamboo shoot and its leaves)*.

With: The panda bear eats bamboo, shoots, and leaves *(meaning the panda bear dines, shoots someone, then leaves)*.

You see how the meaning can be distorted with the wrong punctuation.

A comma is used to separate sentences only if a conjunction or connector is also used. The conjunction and comma work as a team.

Dick hated Friday nights, because they made him lonely.

Sally attended the daily meeting, which always made her cranky.

The problem with the next sentence is *and then*. The toolkit alerts you that using *and then* is wrong. Using *and* with *then* is redundant. *And* implies that two things are simultaneous. *Then* implies one thing happened after the other. Choose one.

Incorrect: Sally tidied her desk, and then she emptied the trashcan.

Correct: Sally tidied her desk and emptied the trashcan.

A comma is not used before *then.* If you use a comma, a squiggly line appears.

Sally tidied her desk, then emptied the trashcan.

Sally tidied her desk then emptied the trashcan.

Comma splices occur when you use a comma instead of a period or semicolon to separate two independent clauses.

Incorrect: Dick opened the drawer, however the gun was missing.

Incorrect: Dick opened the drawer, the gun was gone.

Correct: Dick opened the drawer. However, the gun was missing.

If each clause has a subject and verb, they are technically separate sentences. You can break them up using a period, semi-colon, or colon.

Dick opened the drawer. The gun was gone.

Dick opened the drawer: the gun was gone.

Dick opened the drawer; the gun was gone.

A comma is used when a coordinating conjunction joins two sentences: *and, but, for, or, nor, so,* and *yet.*

Dick needed Sally, yet he was afraid to approach her.

Dick didn't want to attend the meeting, nor did he want to face Sally.

Dick needed Sally, and he dreaded facing her.

Adverbs such as *however* cannot be used to join two independent clauses.

Incorrect: Jane opened the diary, however, the pages were gone.

Correct: Jane opened the diary. However, the pages were gone.

Correct: Jane opened the drawer; however, the pages were gone.

Use commas to separate the base clause from modifying phrases.

Dick opened the diary, removing the pages, hiding them in his coat pocket.

Opening the diary, Dick removed the pages, hiding them in his coat pocket.

Opening the diary, removing the pages, Dick hid them in his coat pocket.

If you add a qualifier or modifier to the beginning or end of a sentence, you need a comma.

Without doubt, Dick is a really fun guy.

Although she knew it was extravagant, Sally couldn't resist buying the new purse.

In order to keep the peace, Dick agreed to go to Maui for a week.

Jane hated her boss, loved the paycheck.

If you insert nonessential words into the middle of sentence, you need to offset them with commas. The best way to tell if the information is nonessential is to read the sentence without the information.

If it can be cut without changing the meaning or direction of the sentence, it needs to be offset with commas.

Dick, who is the committee chairman, will give a presentation at the annual meeting.

It isn't essential that we know Dick is the chairman.

STORY BUILDING BLOCKS III: THE REVISION LAYERS

Dick who was never late didn't show up.

It is essential that we know Dick is never late. If you take out "*who was never late*", then Dick didn't show up. He might have a habit of not showing up and it might not raise any flags. If Dick is punctual and doesn't show up, something is amiss.

Read through your draft with special attention to punctuation, particularly commas. Misplaced commas often let you know that your sentence structure is off. Read it out loud. Does it sound correct?

🖉 Contractions

A contraction is a shortened word or phrase. An apostrophe takes the place of the missing letters.

ain't	he'll	needn't	we'd
aren't	I'd	shan't	we'll
can't	I'll	she'd	we're
couldn't	I'm	she'll	weren't
didn't	isn't	shouldn't	we've
doesn't	it'd	there's	won't
don't	it'll	they'd	wouldn't
'em	it's	they'll	you'd
hadn't	I've	they're	you're
hasn't	let's	they've	you've
he'd	mustn't	wasn't	

Contractions impart tone. They are informal. Writing without them sounds too serious or affected, unless you are writing about a time and place where they weren't in use. You don't have to search and kill all contractions, just make sure you've spread them out and they aren't piled up like road kill on a highway.

✐ Dashes

There are two types of dashes: the en-dash and em-dash. Dashes are often typed as two hyphens, but they are specific ASCII characters. You insert them by clicking on [Insert] [Symbol] [Special Characters] and selecting en-dash or em-dash.

The en-dash separates a range of values, distance, and scores. There are no spaces between the dash and the words it connects.

The car couldn't go more than 25–35 mph.

Dick's Paris–London flight was late.

The en-dash is used in compound adjectives.

Dick launched the surface-to-air missile.

The em-dash—a disruptive punctuation tool—is used to offset a group of words from other words in a sentence or to lead to material at the end of a sentence. It is a mild speed bump.

A sentence can be offset with information prior to the subject and verb, or following the subject and verb. Em-dashes call a great deal of attention to the information in the middle and should be used sparingly.

Dick, the shrewdest sleuth in history, will solve the case.

Dick—the shrewdest sleuth in history—will solve this case.

Dick's investigative skills, his shrewd insight, keen intellect, and creative problem-solving skills, will solve the case.

Dick's investigative skills—his shrewd insight, keen intellect, and creative problem-solving skills—will solve the case.

The em-dashes call attention to the sections in the middle. Em-dashes allow you to insert a sentence within a sentence for effect.

Dick Doe—his enemies call him the silver bullet—solved the case.

The case—Dick called it the toughest of his career—was solved by good detective work.

An em-dash can be used to separate the words at the end of a sentence to show a clean break in continuity.

Dick will be unable to solve the case—unless he has the police department's full cooperation.

Dick's methods have always proven effective—though he never promises a good result.

Em-dashes should be sprinkled sparingly. Two or three times in a manuscript are enough.

✐ Hyphens

The hyphen is a featured key on your keyboard. There is no space between a hyphen and the character on either side of it. Hyphens are used at the end of a sentence to divide words. Most word processing programs are set to do this automatically, particularly when using full justification. You can decide to hyphenate or not hyphenate. The rules for hyphenating at line endings are complicated. Reference a dictionary if you need to. If you adjust one line-break for aesthetic reasons, it may affect subsequent line-breaks in the text.

Compound modifiers need to be hyphenated: *hot-dog-eating contest, five-year-old girl, one-year-old scotch,* and *out-of-date rules.*

All terms based on a single-letter abbreviation should have a hyphen. Technical terms sometimes need hyphens: *A-frame, E-book, E-mail, T-bar, U-boat, U-turn, x-ray.*

Use a hyphen when a prefix comes before a capitalized word or the prefix is capitalized: *non-English.*

Use a hyphen after the prefixes *self, all,* and *ex: all-inclusive, ex-husband,* and *self-control.*

In general, use a hyphen when the prefix ends with the same letter that begins the word: *anti-intellectual* and *de-emphasize*.

There are exceptions: *coordinate, cooperate,* and *unnatural.* When in doubt, look it up.

Use a hyphen with a series of suspended compounds.

Jane needs both full- and part-time employees.

Dick won't babysit two-, three-, or four-year-olds.

This can be annoying, so use it only when you need to and keep the lists short. Hyphens separate compound adjectives before a noun, but not after the noun.

Dick is a well-liked, freedom-loving patriot.

Dick is well liked and freedom loving.

✒ Italics

Italics *emphasize* stuff. The old-fashioned way to format a manuscript required that you underscore the things that are now italicized. Refer to the entity you are submitting to as to whether they want italics within the text or whether they prefer words to be underlined. Italics are usually recognized by the E-book upload services.

Italics are used to set off internal thoughts, dreams, memories, diaries, and journal entries. There are ways to

347

avoid this. Readers dislike reading italics for more than a paragraph or two. Some fonts are not italics friendly.

Italics are used for titles of books, poems, plays, movies, TV shows, magazines, and newspapers.

Dick read the *New York Times*.

Jane read *The Scarlet Letter*.

Dick and Jane went to see *What About Bob* at the theater.

Italics are used for foreign words and phrases unless they have become commonplace, like taco and ciao.

Jane ate *steak au poivre* followed by *crème brûlée*.

Dick did not *parlez* his *Francais*.

Italics are used for emphasis to illustrate contrast, irony, humor, or force.

"Ooh, Jane said she's *angry*."

"I said *sod off*, you twit."

"No, you can't, because *I* said so."

Italics are used for scientific names for genus and species as opposed to the common name.

The gray wolf is a *Canis lupus*.

Puff is a *Felis catus*, or house cat.

Italics can be used for Headers or Footers as a style.

Title of Your Book   *Author Name*

✎ Parentheses

Parentheses offset information you want to de-emphasize or wouldn't normally fit into the sentence. Parentheses interrupt (just like a rude dinner guest). Keep the interruptions to a minimum. Do not use a capital letter for the first item inside the parentheses, even if it's a complete sentence, unless it is a question, exclamation, or proper name.

Long after his retirement, Dick (the one they called the silver bullet) continued to be interested in cases.

Many years ago, Dick Doe (Do you remember him?) solved the most infamous cases in London.

If the information is critical, make it a separate sentence. Don't obscure it with parentheses. If you use parentheses, ask yourself why. Are they really necessary?

Many years ago, Dick Doe solved infamous cases. We used to call him the silver bullet.

✎ Periods, Question Marks, and Exclamation Points

A period indicates that a sentence has ended. There is no space between the period and the last letter of the sentence.

Dick quickly walked down the sidewalk.

A period comes after a number in a list. There is no space between the number and the period. There is a space after the period before the first letter of the list item.

1. Get up.

2. Work all day.

3. Go to bed.

A period is used at the end of a command.

I told Spot to get off of the couch.

A period is used at the end of an indirect question.

Dick asked Jane why she went to the mall after it closed.

Dick asked Sally what she wanted to do.

Dick asked Jane for a date.

Jane wondered if Dick knew Sally cheated on him?

A period is used with abbreviations. When a period follows the abbreviation and the abbreviation is the last word in the sentence, you do not add a second period.

Incorrect: Dick arrived in D.C. at 6:00 p.m..

Correct: Dick arrived in D.C. at 6:00 p.m.

Correct: Did Dick leave Washington D.C.?

Use a question mark if a statement ends in a question.

We can get to D.C. faster, can't we, if we fly?

Dick's question was, how can you end a statement with a question?

Use a question mark at the end of a direct question. You should not combine question marks with exclamation marks. If your writing holds its own, you don't need both.

Why do I have to go to bed early?

Use a question mark with a tag question, which turns a statement into a question. A tag question has a pronoun, helping verb, and a qualifier like *not*. It starts out as a statement and changes into a question.

Dick said, "I told you a million times, did I not?"

Sally said, "Oh that's your angle, is it?"

Jane should quit whining, shouldn't she?

Puff needs to go on a diet, doesn't she?

Dick isn't doing very well, is he?

There were too many cooks in the kitchen, weren't there? (not they!)

Use a question mark at the end of a rhetorical question.

How should Jane have said it, anyway?

Use a question mark after the quotation marks in this sentence.

What if I said, "You've got a situation here"?

Use question marks to emphasize a series of brief questions.

What if the crook targeted your home? Your office? Your car?

Who came up with this idea? The boss? His wife? His secretary?

Use a question mark if it is part of an italicized or underlined title. Do not add a period after this question mark to end the sentence. Do italicize it.

Dick's favorite movie is *Who Slew Auntie Rue?*

If the question mark is not part of a sentence-ending title, don't italicize it.

Did Dick sing *Oh Say Can You See*?

When a question ends with an abbreviation, end the abbreviation with a period then add the question mark.

Didn't he live in Washington, D.C.?

Do not use a question mark if the question is a polite request, especially when the request is long and complex.

Would everyone in this room without a ticket please return to the ticket office and purchase one.

The exclamation point is used to emphasize a statement or commands. Exclamation points are like ALL CAPS, it is shouting. If your dialogue is doing its job, you shouldn't need them. If you use them, do so sparingly!

Sally said, "No!"

"Puff, get off of that counter now!"

If you use an exclamation you don't need to follow it up with a dialogue tag that performs the same function.

Incorrect: "Puff, get off of that counter now!" Jane yelled.

Correct: "Puff, get off of that counter now," Jane yelled.

Correct: "Puff, get off of that counter now!" Jane clapped her hands.

✏ Semi-Colons

353

A semicolon separates two ideas or sentences to show a relationship between the two. A semicolon is often followed by a connector. The second sentence should modify the understanding of the first.

The following examples could easily be divided into two short sentences. So why use a semicolon? A semicolon expresses a close relationship between the two sentences in which removing one would change the meaning of the other.

Dick is a funny guy; he has no choice.

If you removed *he has no choice*, Dick would just be a funny guy. The second sentence implies that he is forced to be funny.

Dick is a funny guy; however, his humor can be offensive.

If you removed the second sentence, Dick would still be a funny guy, but the reader would not know that this humor can be offensive.

Dick needed to find Sally; he had to warn her.

If you removed the second sentence, you don't know why Dick has to find Sally. He could have good news for her rather than a warning.

A period between the two sentences would make the reader stop for second. The semicolon makes them pause, allowing the connection to sink in. Use semicolons for effect and intentionally. They add variation to your sentences. To use a semicolon, both sentences must have a subject and verb.

If you connect two sentences with a conjunction (*and, but, or*) you do not need a semicolon.

Dick ran down the alley and he stopped outside the door.

If the second sentence begins with a connector (*however, therefore, nevertheless*), you must use a semicolon to connect the two.

Dick is a funny guy; however, his humor borders on the tasteless.

Jane is a sweet girl; therefore, she is easy to fool.

You cannot glue two sentences together with a comma. That is a comma splice and it confuses the reader.

Jane was quite upset at the party, she felt she was being ignored.

Sally is a hard worker, she averages twelve hours a day.

Each of the comma splices could be fixed by separating the sentences with a period, semicolon, or conjunction.

Jane was quite upset at the party. She felt she was being ignored.

Jane was quite upset at the party; she felt she was being ignored.

Jane was quite upset at the party because she felt she was being ignored.

The only exception to the comma splice is if you have a list of items that could stand alone as full sentences. The commas can attach the items as long as it is clear that the list is of relatively equal items.

Dick opened his desk drawer, he took the gun from the drawer, and he concealed the gun in his coat pocket.

The list illustrates the step-by-step process which renders the splices acceptable as a cumulative sentence. The sentence could be tightened.

Dick opened the desk drawer, removed the gun, and hid it in his pocket.

Another use for the semicolon is when you have a complex sentence with multiple commas. You need to make sure your paragraphs are easy to follow. Otherwise, the reader gets lost.

This happens if you have too many commas. In instances where all the commas are necessary, some can be replaced with semicolons.

Dick's company has branches in four cities: Akron, Ohio, Hershey, Pennsylvania, Lexington, Kentucky, and Indianapolis, Indiana.

You could clarify this sentence by using semicolons:

Dick's company has branches in four cities: Akron, Ohio; Hershey, Pennsylvania; Lexington, Kentucky; and Indianapolis, Indiana.

This should be a rare occurrence, particularly in fiction writing.

✐ Slashes or Slant marks

A forward slash or slant mark indicates a choice between the words it separates. If you can replace the slash with the word *or*, it is correct. There is no space between the slash and the letters on either side of it.

The psychology class grade will be a pass/fail.

I hate having to use his/her to be politically correct.

A slash or slant mark is used with fractions.

Jane finished 1/3 to 1/2 of her manuscript.

A slash or slant mark is used with dates.

Schedules are available for the 2003/4 school year.

We will have the meeting on 12/12/2012.

A slash or slant mark is used to replace a hyphen to join two words or abbreviations.

AC/DC

w/o

on/off switch

A slash can indicate a line-break in poetry. A space should separate the slash from both words.

Gaily bedight / a gallant knight / in sunshine and in shadow

A slash is used in a website address. There are no spaces in between.

https://www.dianahurwitz. com

A backslash indicates a pathway and is used primarily in computing.

C:\program files\Word

Revision Tips

✍ This layer can be done on the printed version as one of your final rounds. Do a search and kill for the rarer symbols such as parenthesis, brackets, colons, and semicolons. Don't do a search for commas and periods.

✍ Are all punctuation marks used correctly?

✍ Do you need that particular type of punctuation in that sentence? Does it serve a valid purpose?

Diana Hurwitz

USE THIS NOT THAT

The following is a list of commonly misused words. There are many more. Add your favorites. Make sure all of these words are used and spelled correctly. Spell Check will not recognize misused words.

a/an: Use *a* before a word that starts with a consonant sound and *an* before a word that starts with a vowel sound.

a lot/plethora: *A lot* means many. *Plethora* means too many. *Alot* is not a word.

accept/except: *Accept* means to receive an item or realize you can't change something. *Except* is a modifying connector that means *to exclude*.

accidently/incidentally: *Accidentally* means to do something by mistake. *Incidentally* means *by the way* and directs the focus to a new topic.

accidently/accidentally: *Accidently* is a variant. The standard is *accidentally*.

adapt/adopt: *Adapt* means shift to accommodate. *Adopt* means to take something on (like a policy or the care of a child).

addict/attic/edict: An *addict* takes drugs. An *attic* stores trunks. An *edict* is an order.

addition/edition: An *addition* is something you add. An *edition* is something you publish.

adverse/averse: *Adverse* means conditions are bad. *Averse* means you don't like something.

advice/advise: *Advice* is something you give someone. It is a noun. *Advise* is something you do to someone. It is a verb.

affect/effect: *Affect* is a verb. *Affect* is also a psychological term that means someone's appearance. *Effect* is almost always used as a noun, but is sometimes used as a verb.

agree with/agree to: You can *agree to* (*comply with*) something without *agreeing with* (*supporting the premise of*) the person asking you to do it.

all ready/already: *All ready* means prepared. *Already* is an adverb meaning previously done.

allusion/illusion: An *allusion* (*verb: alluded*) refers to something that exists. *Illusion* refers to something that doesn't.

alright/all right: *All right* is considered correct. *Alright* is used but isn't a proper word.

among/between: *Among* indicates more than one thing. *Between* indicates two things.

amoral/immoral/immortal: *Amoral* means morally ambivalent. *Immoral* means morally wrong. *Immortal* means to live forever.

anxious/eager: *Anxious* means worried. *Eager* means looking forward to something.

because of/due to: *Because of* explains why. *Due to* points to a noun (*person, place, or thing*).

because/since: *Because* explains why. *Since* explains why or refers to time. Read the sentence. Does the phrase define why or when?

can/may: *Can* refers to the ability to do something. *May* refers to permission to do something.

capital/capitol: *Capital* is something you invest, a type of letter, or a city. *Capitol* is a building that houses government.

cite/sight/site: To *cite* something is to repeat it. To *sight* something is to see it. *Site* is noun indicating a location.

complement/compliment: A *complement* completes something. A *compliment* is praise.

conscience/conscious: *Conscience* tells you if you are doing right or wrong. *Conscious* is being awake and aware.

continual/continuous: *Continual* means it happens repeatedly, with or without interruption. *Continuous* means it happens without interruption.

convince/persuade: *Convince* means to bring someone around to your way of thinking. *Persuasion* means coercing someone into doing what you want.

could of/would of/should of: These are inaccurate. *Could've, would've, should've,* and *coulda, woulda, shouda* are incorrect too. Use *could have, would have,* and *should have.*

cue/queue: A *cue* is a signal. A *queue* is a line.

disinterested/uninterested: *Disinterested* means impartial. *Uninterested* means you don't care.

e.g./i.e.: The abbreviation *e.g.* stands for *exempli gratia,* which means *for example.* It is followed by an example. The abbreviation *i.e.* stands for *id est,* which means *that is to say.* It is followed by an explanation.

ellipse/ellipsis: An *ellipse* is a geometric shape. Ellipsis is a typographic series of dots (...).

ensure/insure: These are used interchangeably. However, *ensure* means to make certain and *insure* means to take out a policy.

etc./et. al. *Etc.* is the abbreviation for *et cetera,* which means *the rest* or *so forth.* It is used in reference to things and implies that the list is incomplete or information is left out. *Et. al.* is the abbreviation for *et alia* and means *and others*. This is used in reference to people.

flesh out/flush out: If you flesh something out, you expand it or fill it in. If you flush it out, you get rid of it. You *flesh* out a sketch. You *flush* out a drain.

good/well: *Good* is an adjective. *Well* is an adverb. If someone asks you how you are, you are doing *well*. If someone asks you how you are at golf, you are *good*.

historical/historic: *Historic* is something that stands the test of time. *Historical* means it happened in the past and is part of the study of history.

home/homing/hone/honing: To *hone* is to sharpen. To *hone in on* means to focus on. *Home* is where you live. A *homing* pigeon is a bird that returns to the same place frequently.

indolent/insolent: *Indolent* means lazy. *Insolent* means rude and disrespectful.

ingenuous ingenious: *Ingenuous* means naive. *Ingenious* means clever.

juxtaposition: means that two opposite things are happening at the same time. It does not mean two items are lined up side by side.

into/in to: *Into* is a preposition linking a verb to a place. You drop cookies *into* a jar. You walk *in to* a bar get a drink.

it's/its: *It's* means it is. *Its* means it belongs to.

irregardless/regardless: *Irregardless* is not standard. The prefix *ir* cancels out the *regardless*. It's a double negative. *Regardless* is preferred.

lie/lay: *Lie* is something you do (stretch out on a bed or tell a fib). *Lay* is something you to do something else and requires an object.

literally/metaphorically: *Literally* is what is actually done. *Metaphorically* is what you wish you could have done.

me/I: You should always put the other person first: Dick and I, Sally and I, or you and me.

moot/mute: *Moot* means zero value. *Mute* means no volume.

nauseated/nauseous/nauseating: *Nauseated* means suffering from nausea. *Nauseous* and *nauseating* mean inducing nausea.

orient/orientate: *Orient* is American English. The Brits use *orientate*. Both are correct. If you aren't British, use orient.

passed/past: *Passed* is the past tense of *to pass*, meaning to give something to someone. *Past* refers to a prior time.

penultimate/ultimate: *Penultimate* means second to last. *Ultimate* means top of the pile.

precede/proceed: *Precede* means to come before. *Proceed* means to move forward or financial earnings.

principle/principal: *Principle* means primary or a moral position. A *principal* runs a school.

racked/wracked: A rack is a shelving unit or a torture device. To wrack is to damage or destroy. You rack your brain.

respectfully/respectively: *Respectfully* means doing something with consideration. *Respectively* means *according to each*.

stationary/stationery: *Stationery* is something you write on. *Stationary* means standing still.

that/which: *That* connects an essential clause to a sentence. *Which* adds a clause with extraneous information that could be cut without hurting the sentence.

that/who: If you are talking about people, use *who*. If you are talking about things, use *that*. The spell checker tells you to use *that* for characters instead of *who*.

then/than: *Then* indicates time. *Than* indicates a comparison.

they/it: *They* implies a group of people or things. *It* implies a thing. A collective noun such as *company* is an *it*.

three-hundred-and-sixty-degree turn: Three-hundred and sixty degrees is a full circle. One-hundred and eighty degrees is a half-turn, ninety-degrees degrees is a quarter-turn, and forty-five is an eighth of a turn. How far did your character really turn?

times bigger/times faster/times smaller: All are incorrect. It should be *three times as big, three times better,* and *three times as large.*

to/too/two: *To* is a direction. *Too* means *also.* Two is a number.

toward/towards: Both are correct. Towards is British or Southern.

was/were: Statements require the indicative verb form. If you have a singular noun, you use the singular verb *was.* If you use a plural noun, you use the plural verb *were.* The subjunctive form of the verb is used for wishes, suggestions, hypothetical musings, or conditions rather than stating a fact. It sounds awkward to most ears: *I wish I were in Maui.*

whether/weather: *Whether* is a conjunction. *Weather* is snow and rain.

Revision Tips

✍ Do a search for the above words. Did you use the correct word? If not, change it.

✍ When you do a final proofreading pass, make sure the words are spelled correctly.

REPETITIVE WORDS

Oh, repetitive words, how I hate them. However, searching for and killing them is essential to tightening your manuscript. All writers have favorites. My list changes with every book. These are the pet words, phrases, and verbs that our minds grab in the moment. At the end of the manuscript, we realize that we have used them fifty times.

I can't account for everyone's favorites here, but I do offer a few. Add your darling bugaboos to the list or make a list of your own. If a descriptive word or phrase is used multiple times, see if you can get it down to only a few instances per manuscript.

Some words have to be repeated such as: *a, he, I, me, we, she, and, but, do, does, the, am, were,* and *is.* Don't do a search for them. The results would be astronomic. When proofreading, do pay attention to how many times these simple words appear within the same sentence and paragraph. Tighten your sentences where possible. Try to avoid starting out two consecutive sentences or paragraphs with the same word.

Actually

absolutely	exactly	really
categorically	genuinely	surely
conclusively	in fact	truly
de facto	in reality	unambiguously
decidedly	in truth	unconditionally
decisively	indeed	unquestionably
definitely	literally	veritably
doubtless	positively	very
easily	precisely	

Appear

arise	come out	present
arrive	crop up	recur
attend	develop	rise
be present	drop in	roll in
blow in	expose	show
bob up	issue	show up
break through	loom	spring
breeze in	make it	surface
check in	materialize	tune in
clock in	occur	turn out
come	pop in	turn up
come forth	pop up	

Arrogant

aloof	cool	peremptory
assuming	disdainful	pompous
audacious	domineering	presumptuous
autocratic	ego trip	pretentious
bossy	egotistic	proud
bragging	haughty	puffed up
cavalier	high-handed	scornful
cheeky	imperious	self-important
cocky	insolent	smarty
cold shoulder	know it all	smug
concealed	lordly	snippy
contemptuous	overbearing	snooty

snotty   superior   vain
stuck-up   swaggering
supercilious   uppity

At least

at best   inadequately   notably
at most   incompletely   noticeably
at worst   insufficiently   partially
by degree   measurably   piecemeal
carelessly   not entirely   relatively
halfway   not fully   slightly
in part   not wholly   somewhat

Bag

attaché   handbag   purse
backpack   haversack   rucksack
briefcase   hold-all   sack
carry-on   kit   saddlebag
carry-all   knapsack   satchel
clutch   pack   suitcase
duffle   packet   tote
gear   pocket
grub bag   pocketbook

Beyond

above   farther   over
after   further   past
ahead   free of   remote
apart from   hyper   superior to
before   more   without
behind   remote   yonder
besides   moreover
clear of   outside

Bile: (limit to once or twice)   acid   food

Breeze: air   current   gale   gust   hurricane   wind

371

Body parts

abrasion
ankle
arm
artery
back
bones
brain
bowels
brow
bruise
buttocks
cheek
chest
chin
ear
elbow
eyebrow
eyes
face
feet
fingers
foot
forehead
frown
gaze
glance
grimace
grin
gut
hair
hand
head
heart
hip
instep
jaw
joint
jowl
knee
knuckle
lips
lungs
mouth
muscle
nails
nape
nose
leg
lobe
look
orbit
paunch
pinky
ribs
scab
scalp
scapula
shoulder
shin
shrug
side
sigh
smile
spine
stomach
teeth
tendon
thigh
tissue
toe
tongue
vein
vessel
wound

Bully

annoy
antagonize
bludgeon
bluster
browbeat
bulldoze
coerce
cow
despot
domineer
dragoon
enforce
force
harass
harry
hector
insolent
intimidate
lean on
lord over
menace
oppress
overbear
persecute
pest
push around
rascal
ride roughshod
rowdy
ruffian
showboat
swagger
tease
terrorize
threaten
torment
torture
tough
tyrannize

Cheater

bluff	dodger	quack
charlatan	double-crosser	rascal
chiseler	double-dealer	rogue
con man	enticer	scammer
confidence man	take	shark
conniver	hypocrite	sharper
cozener	imposter	shyster
crook	jockey	swindler
deceiver	knave	trickster
decoy	masquerader	
defrauder	pretender	

Come to

arrive	crop up	meet
befall	emerge from	occur
betide	fall out	stumble on
blunder on	go	transpire
break	hit upon	tumble
bump	light	turn up
come about	light upon	
come off	luck	

Dark

darkened	ill-lit	shaded
dim	indistinct	shadowy
dingy	inky	shady
drab	lurid	somber
dull	misty	sooty
dun	murky	stygian
dusk	nebulous	sunless
dusky	obscure	tenebrous
faint	opaque	unlighted
foggy	overcast	unlit
gloomy	pitch-black	vague
grimy	pitch-dark	
ill-lighted	pitchy	

Dart

dash	hurry	rush	spring
flash	hurtle	sail	sprint
fling	launch	scamper	spurt
flit	move	scoot	start
float	quickly	scud	tear
fly	pitch	scurry	throw
gallop	plunge	shoot	thrust
hasten	propel	skim	
heave	run	speed	

Decided

adjudge	conjecture	gather	resolve
adjudicated	decree	guess	rule
agree	determine	judge	select
award	elect	mediate	set
call shots	end	opt	surmise
choose	establish	pick	tap
cinch	figure	poll	vote
commit	fix upon	purpose	will
oneself	form an	reach a	
conclude	opinion	decision	

Deep

abysmal	buried	low rooted
abyss	deep-seated	submarine
abyssal	distant	submerged
below	down-reaching	subterranean
beneath	far	sunk
bottomless	fathomless	underground
broad	immersed	unfathomable

Depart

all out	clear out	flee	for it
all the way	debark	head out	make scarce
at a good clip	decamp	hightail	make tracks
beat it	disappear	in full gallop	runaway
bolt	escape	lickety-split	scram
break camp	evacuate	make a break	skedaddle

slip away	vamoose		

Dip

	dunk	scoop	

Drizzle

distill	gush	salivate	sprinkle
drip	inundate	seep	squirt
drivel	leak	slaver	stream
drool	ooze	slobber	swamp
drop	pour	splash	trill
flood	run	spout	weep

Eerie

awful	fearful	nasty	superstitious
awesome	frightening	nightmarish	terrifying
bizarre	ghostly	ominous	threatening
crawly	ghoulish	scary	uncanny
creepy	gruesome	shuddery	unearthly
direful	hair-raising	sinister	unpleasant
disgusting	horrible	spectral	weird
disturbing	macabre	spooky	
dreadful	menacing	strange	
fantastic	mysterious	supernatural	

Empty-handed

beggared	devoid	minus	stripped
deprived	dispossessed	robbed	wanting
destitute	divested	shorn	without

Extract

avulse	elicit	garner	reap
bring out	eradicate	get	secure
catheterize	evoke	glean	select
cull	evulsion	obtain	separate
derive	exact	pick up	siphon
distill	express	pluck	squeeze
draw	extirpate	press out	take
draw out	extort	pry	tear
eke out	extricate	pull	uproot

weed out
withdraw

wrest
wring

yank

Faced

accost
address
affront
annoy
bother
brave
challenge

confront
cross
dare
defy
encounter
entice
faced

down
flout
greet
hail
meet
oppose
proposition

repel
resist
salute
scorn
tell off
welcome
withstand

Ferocious

barbaric
barbarous
bloodthirsty
brutal
brutish
cruel
feral

fierce
frightful
inhuman
man eating
merciless
murderous
pitiless

predatory
rapacious
ravening
ravenous
relentless
ruthless
savage

untamed
vehement
vicious
voracious
wild
wolfish

Fog

becloud
bedim
befog
blear
blind
darken
daze

dazzle
dim
glare
gloom
haze
mask
miasma

muddy
murk
murkiness
nebula
obscure
shade
smog

smoke
steam
vapor
wisp

Foliage

ash
bracken
branches
brier
brush
brushwood
burr
bushes

canopy
catch weed
clearing
coppice
copse
cover
dell
dingle

elm
fern
forest
glen
gorse
grove
hedge
hill

hillock
hollow
leaves
limbs
maple
meadow
nettle
oak

pine	sage brush	thicket	underbrush
prickly	scrub	thistle	undergrowth
shrub	shrubbery	thorn	valley
redwood	spinney	trees	wood
roots	spray	twigs	

Glance

angry stare	gawk	look daggers	squint
bald eye	gaze	menace	stare
black look	glare	peek	swivel
dog eye	glimpse	peep	whither
fleeting look	glower	peer	
gander	hawk	pierce	
gape	look	scowl	

Go

abscond	get going	move out	set off
approach	get lost	near	shove off
beat it	get off	pass	skip out
bug out	going	proceed	split
cruise	hie	progress	take flight
decamp	hightail	pull out	take leave
depart	journey	push off	take off
escape	lam	push on	tool
exit	leave	quit	travel
fare	light out	repair	vamoose
flee	make for	retire	wend
fly	mosey	run along	withdraw
get away	move	run away	

Good

acceptable	exceptional	great	precious
admirable	favorable	honorable	prime
agreeable	first class	marvelous	satisfactory
commendable	first rate	pleasing	splendid
excellent	gratifying	positive	super

Grab

bag	grasp	nab	snatch
capture	grip	pluck	spirit away
carry off	hook	remove	steal away
catch	kidnap	seize	take
clutch	land	shanghai	
corral	latch on	snag	
grapple	make off with	snap up	

Halt

adjourn	cease fire	hold back	stand still
arrest	check	impede	stay
balk	curb	intermit	stern
bar	desist	interrupt	stop
block	deter	obstruct	suspend
break	draw up	pause	terminate
into	drop anchor	pull up	wait
break off	end	punctuate	
can it	frustrate	rest	
cease	hamper	stall	

Howl

bark	groan	roar	weep
brawl	growl	scream	whimper
bay	hoot	shout	whine
bellow	keen	shriek	woof
blubber	lament	snap	yell
clamor	moan	snarl	yelp
cry	outcry	ululate	yip
clamor	quest	wail	yowl

Idiot

ass	donkey	half-wit	ninny	simpleton
blockhead	dumb ox	ignoramus	nitwit	stupid
booby	dumbbell	imbecile	pinhead	tomfool
cretin	dunce	jackass	pointy	twit
dimwit	dunderhead	jerk	head	
	fool			

Inch   crept   crawled   slid

Indicate

designate   highlight   signal   suggest

Join

abut	catch up	converge	draw near
accompany	close in	creep up	loom
assemble	contact	crowd	

Jump

bob	drop	leaping	spring
bounce	fall	lurch	start
bound	gambol	nosedive	swerve
buck	hop	plummet	twitch
canter	hurdle	plunge	upspring
caper	jar	pounce	upsurge
capriole	jerk	rise	vault
dance	jolt	shock	wrench
dive	leapfrog	skip	

Just

absolutely	by then	most	recently
about	close to	much	relatively
about to	close upon	near to	right
accurately	completely	nearly	right now
all but	directly	nigh on	once
altogether	earlier	not quite	roughly
approximately	entirely	now	scarce
around	essentially	perfectly	scarcely
as good as	even now	practically	sharp
as close to	exactly	precisely	substantially
at present	expressly	presently	totally
before	formerly	pretty near	utterly
before now	fully	previously	virtually
bordering on	heretofore	purely	well-nigh
by now	in effect	quite	wholly

Kill

annihilate	exterminate	strangle
asphyxiate	exsanguinate	suffocate
assassinate	murder	take
butcher	poison	waste
eradicate	slaughter	winterkill
execute	slay	wipeout

Laugh

giggle	guffaw	hoot	holler	snort

Leave

beat it	get off	make progress	start
blow	go	pass	take off
continue	go away	proceed	travel
depart	hie	pull out	wend
exit	journey	push on	withdraw
fare	keep going	quit	
get away	launch	repair to	
get lost	light out	shove off	

Liar

blackguard	delinquent	ruffian	varmint
bully	fraud	scoundrel	villain
bum	hypocrite	sneak	wastrel
cad	pretender	swindler	wretch
cardsharp	robber	tough	
charlatan	rogue	tramp	
cheat	rowdy	trickster	

Look

admire	flash	mark	pore over
attend	focus	mind	read
behold	gape	note	regard
beware	gawk	notice	scan
consider	gaze	observe	scout
contemplate	glance	ogle	scrutinize
eye	heed	peep	see
eyeball	inspect	peer	spot

spy	study	trend	watch
stare	survey	view	

Murky

black	dusk	lowering	sad
brackish	dusky	misty	shadowy
charcoal	ebon	mucky	smoky
cloudy	ebony	muddy	somber
dark	filthy	nasty	sooty
darkened	foggy	nebulous	squalid
dim	foul	opaque	starless
dingy	fuzzy	overcast	stormy
dismal	gloomy	pitch	swarthy
drab	gray	dark	unclear
dreary	impenetrable	raven	turbid
dull	ink-like	roily	veiled
dun	inky	sable	

Nod

acknowledge	bend	duck	salute
acquiesce	bob	greet	say yes
agree	bow	incline	sign
approve	consent	indicate	signal
assent	curtsy	permission	tip the head
beckon	dip	respond	

Nothing

naught	nonentity	squat	zippo
nil	nothingness	void	
nobody	naught	zilch	
none	nullity	zip	

Perhaps

apparently	imaginably	no doubt	practically
assuredly	like	perchance	presumably
believably	enough	perhaps	presumptively
doubtless	maybe	plausibly	reasonably
expediently	most likely	possibly	seemingly

Point

aim	head	make	tab
beam	hint	name	tag
cast	imply	offer	tend
denote	indicate	peg	train
designate	influence	pin down	turn
direct	lay	signify	zero in
face	lead	slant	
finger	level	steer	
guide	look	suggest	

Push

accelerate	dragoon	jostle	railroad
achieve	drive	key up	ram
advance	effort	kid	rest on
assault	egg on	launch	sell on
attack	elbow	lean	shove
bearing	elevate	lie on	speed up
bear down	encourage	mass	spur
blow	energy	motivate	squash
bring forward	exert	move	squeeze
browbeat	expedite	nudge	squish
buck	fire up	oblige	skyrocket
budge	force	offensive	stave off
bulldoze	forge ahead	onset	steamroll
bump	goad	overbear	stir
butt	goose	persuade	storm
charge	hasten	poke	strain
coerce	high pressure	press	strong-arm
come forward	hurry	pressure	thrust
conquer	hustle	prod	turn aside
constrain	impact	progress	turn away
continue	impel	promote	turn on
crowd	influence	propulsion	turn off
crush	inspire	push	urge
depress	jolly	push ahead	ward off
dig	jolt	push on	
dispatch	jam	quicken	

Quick

apace	hastily	instantaneously	speedy
brisk	hurriedly	promptly	swift
expeditious	immediately	pronto	swiftly
flat out	in a flash	rapid	
full tilt	in haste	speedily	

Retreat

back down	hesitate	stop
back up	recede	withdraw
halt	reverse	yield

Rise

ascend	stood	surmount	turn out
climb	straighten	sweep	up
rose	surface	upward	upspring
sprout	surge	tower	

Roar

bank	brawl	grunt	thunder
bawl	bray	holler	trumpet
bay	clamor	howl	vociferate
bellow	crash	rumble	yell
blast	cry	shout	woof
bluster	explode	sound	yap
boom	growl	snarl	yip

Rock

bedrock	jagged	petrified	slab
boulder	lava	promontory	slag
cobblestone	lithic	quarry	solid
crag	lodge	reef	stone
crust	mass	rough	thrum
earth	monolith	rubble	
gravel	pebble	shelf	

383

Roll

arch	drive	spiral	undulate
bend	eddy	swing around	wheel
bind	pirouette	swirl	whirl
bow	pivot	swivel	wind
bowl	reel	trundle	wrap
circle	rock	turn	
coil	rotate	twirl	
curve	spin	twist	

Rustle

crackle	crush	flutter	whisper
crinkle	flap	susurrus	

Said

accounted	decided	held	supposed
alleged	deemed	reckoned	thought
assumed	determined	regarded	
conjectured	estimated	reported	
considered	gossiped	rumored	

Scramble

clamber	jostle	push	scurry
climb	make	run	scuttle
crawl	haste	rush	struggle
hasten	move	scrabble	vie

Seem

assume	imply	manifest	sounds like
display	indicate	present	strike as
evidence	insinuate	pretend	suggest
exhibit	look	resemble	
express	look like	show	
hint	make clear	sounds	

Shallow

bank	insubstantial	slight	trivial
hollow	sand bar	superficial	unsound
inconsequential	shelf	surface	
inconsiderable	shoal	trifling	

Shiver

chill	quiver	thrill	tremble
frisson	shake	throb	
quake	shudder	tingle	

Shrew

backbiter	hellion	siren	vituperator
fury	hussy	spitfire	vixen
harpy	nag	termagant	wench
harridan	porcupine	tigress	
hell cat	she-wolf	virago	

Shrug

bow	motion	shrug	wave
curtsy	nod	signal	wink
gesture	salute	token	

Silence

deafened	quiet	shut up	stillness
hush	sh	silent	
mute	shush	still	

Sit

be seated	install	pose	sat
bear on	lie	posture	seat
cover	park	relax	seat oneself
ensconce	perch	remain	settle
hunker	plop down	rest	squat

Slid

coast	drop	glide	propel
drift	fall	launch	sag
drive	fell	move	scooted

385

shift skate skim tumble
shove skid slip

Slither

angle grovel prowl squirm
bank hang back scrabble steal
bow hook sidle undulate
clamber inch skitter wind
coast lag skulk worm
cower lurk slid wriggle
curve meander slide writhe
drag notch slip zigzag
flex pass quietly slither
fork plod snake
glide poke sneak

Slow

amble easily lethargically saunter
calmly gradually linger slowly
comfortably inactively lingeringly sluggishly
composedly indolently listlessly stroll
delay laggardly loiter tardily
deliberately languidly meander traipse
dilatorily languorously mope unhurriedly
drift lazily ramble without haste

Smell (bad)

aroma malodorous reek scent
fetid odiferous ripe stench
fume odor rotting stink

Smile

beam grin look happy sniggle
cackle guffaw look pleased titter
chortle laugh simper
crow look amused smirk
exult look delighted snicker

Sneer

affront	dig	lampoon	scorn
belittle	disdain	laugh at	slam
brick bat	disparage	leer	slight
burlesque	dump	mock	smile
caricature	flout	put down	sneeze at
condemn	gibe	quip	sniff at
crack	gird	rally	snigger
curl lip	grin	rank out	swipe
decry	insult	ridicule	taunt
deride	jeer	satirize	
detract	jest	scoff	

Snicker

bray	guffaw	smirk	tee hee
chortle	hee-haw	sneer	titter
chuckle	knock	snigger	
giggle	mock	sniggle	

Stalk

ambush	haunt	shadow	tail
chase	hunt	stride	track
drive	pace	strut	trail
flush out	pursue	swagger	

Start

commence	incite	issue	set out
depart	initiate	kick off	set up
embark	instigate	launch	spring
get going	institute	sally forth	turn on
go ahead	introduce	set about	undertake

Sudden

abrupt	now	swift	without delay
at once	quickly	unexpected	without
directly	right away	unanticipated	warning
instantly	straight away	unaware	

Tendril

airy	fibrous	plait	tiffany
braid	filament	ring	transparent
circle	fine	roll	turn
cobweb	flimsy	scroll	twine
corkscrew	gossamer	sheer	twirl
curl	light	silky	twist
delicate	loop	spiral	whorl
diaphanous	pigtail	thin	wind

Thankful

beholden	gratified	obliged	relieved
content	indebted	overwhelmed	satisfied
grateful	much obliged	pleased	

Triumphant

boastful	exultant	jubilant	winning
celebratory	glorious	proud	
conquering	happy	swaggering	
elated	high	victorious	

Turn

about face	detour	relapse	subvert
aim	deviation	retrace	swing
alter	digress	return	swirl
alternate	diverge	revert	switch
angle	double back	pirouette	tack
backside	face about	pivot	twist
bend	flexure	reverse	upset
bow	fork	roll	vary
branch	go back	rotate	veer
call off	incline	round	volte-face
capsize	inverse	sheer	wheel
change	invert	shift	whip
circle	loop	shunt	whirl
convert	move	shy away	wind
curve	re-channel	sidetrack	winding
cycle	recoil	spin	yaw
depart	regress	spiral	zigzag

Vomit

belch	expel	interrupt	spew
bring up	gag	lose it	spit up
discharge	give off	puke	throw up
disgorge	gush	regurgitate	upchuck
dry heave	heave	repeat	vent
emit	hiccup	retch	
erupt	hurl	ruminate	

Walk

accompany	go	promenade	stroll
advance	hike	race	strut
amble	hoof it	ramble	stump
ambulate	jaunt	roam	toddle
airing	legwork	rove	tour
ankle	lumber	run	traipse
boot	march	saunter	tramp
canter	meander	scuff	traverse
carriage	pace	shamble	tread
circuit	pad	schlep	trek
constitutional	parade	shuffle	troop
escort	patrol	slog	trudge
exercise	perambulate	stalk	turn
file	peregrination	step	wander
foot it	plod	stretch	
gait	prance	stride	

Warm

affectionate	fond	tepid
ardent	tender	

Watch

attend	eye	note	probe
case	follow	notice	pry
check out	gaze	observe	regard
concentrate	inspect	pay	scan
consider	look	attention	scope
contemplate	mark	peer	scour
examine	mind	penetrate	scrutinize

see
spy
stake out

stare
study
survey

take in
take notice
view

wait

Wave

beachcomber
beckon
bending
billow
breaker
coil
comber
convolution
corkscrew
crest
crush
curl
curlicue
current
drift
falter
flap
flood
flourish
flow
fluctuate
flutter

fly
foam
gesticulate
ground swell
gush
heave
indicate
influx
loop
motion
movement
oscillate
outbreak
palpitate
pulsate
pulse
quaver
quiver
rash
reel
ridge
ripple

rippling
rocking
roll
roller
rush
scroll
see-saw
shake
sign
signal
stream
stir
stream
surge
sway
sweep
swell
swing
swirl
swish
switch
swoosh

tendency
tide
tremble
tube
twirl
twist
undulation
unevenness
uprising
upsurge
vacillate
vibrate
wag
waggle
waver
whirl
wield
wigwag
wobble
white cap
winding

Woods

brake
bramble
briar
brush
chaparral
chase
clump

coppice
cover
covert
creeper
forest
grove
growth

hedge
hinterland
jungle
park
planting
scrub
scrubland

shrubbery
stand
thicket
tundra
woodland

FORMATTING FOR

PRINT & E-BOOKS

Always make a copy of your manuscript before you reformat it. Keep the original, edited version intact. The following suggestions are for *Word for Windows*. It is important that you save it as **.doc** not **.docx**. Other word processing programs have different menu options and layouts, but the theory is the same. The first part is for a basic manuscript that you wish to submit to an agent or editor. We will explore e-book formatting later on.

To begin, save a new copy of your manuscript. For *Word 1993-2007* Go to the [Word] icon on the top left. Click on [Word Options] in the bottom right corner. For *Word 2010* click on the File tab.

Click on [Proofing] then [Auto Correct Options]. Turn them all off. Save then exit.

A quick way to make sure all formatting is erased is to select "all" by using [CTRL] [A]. Go to the top tool bar and click on the [Aa]+eraser icon which clears all formatting. You may lose some page breaks and returns. That's okay. As you read through the manuscript, insert the correct formatting, remove unintentional spaces, add necessary indents, etc. It is a headache, but you'll avoid embarrassing format glitches. Your agent or editor will thank you for it.

This basic information comes with the caveat that some agents or editors want something slightly different. They may want Arial instead of Times New Roman. They may want single space instead of double space. Special formatting can be lost when you e-mail content.

There are different rules for each E-book upload service if you choose to publish your work yourself.

In either case, you should save a copy of your manuscript as *Title - for Agent/Editor* before changing the format. That way, you maintain standard formatting in the original and you won't be confused about which version to send out to the agent or editor.

The danger is when you find errors as you go along and change them in one version, but forget to change them in the other versions. Take notes as to the page number, change made, and a few words surrounding the error.

Page 54, change *trash* to *treasure*, Dick found trash at the dig site.

You can open your source and alternate documents and make the same corrections. This is made easier by using [Control] [F] or Find. Enter a few words into the search box rather than one. Entering one word gives you multiple options to look at. Entering five or six words should give you the entry you need.

[Control] [Find] [Dick found trash at]

It's tempting to tweaks words, even rewrite entire paragraphs, as you go along. Restrain yourself. Heavy revision requires you to proofread your entire manuscript all over again.

If you absolutely must make a significant revision, remember to make the exact change to your other copies. If you do large-scale revision, erase all the other versions and reformat the new version of the manuscript for each entity to avoid confusion.

This is particularly important if you are formatting a version for print and a version for E-book. You don't want significantly different versions of your work out there.

Formatting for Agents & Editors

▤ **Page Format:** Your page should be set up with the following basic parameters.

☒ Click on [Home]. Expand [Font]. Change the following fields:

Font: Times New Roman

Font Style: leave blank

Font Size: 12 (You can change Chapter Headings to 14 pt)

Font Color: Black or Default (default should be black!)

Underline Style: None

☒ Click on [Page Layout] then expand [Page Setup]. Change the following fields:

Margins: 1 inch all around.

Gutter: 0

☒ Click on [Page Layout], expand [Paragraph]. Change the following fields:

Indentation Left and Right: 0

Indentation Special: First line by 0.50

Alignment: Left (not justified!)

Line Spacing: Double

Outline level: Body Text

📄 **Title Page**

Upper left hand corner: Author's real name, address, phone, fax, email, and word count based on the word count tool on *Word* or whatever method the entity you are submitting to prefers.

They may use a specific formula such as 250 words per page.

Jane Doe
123 ABC Lane
Anywhere, USA 11111
(888) 888-8888
janedoe@yahoo.com
www.janedoe.com
55,000 words

Center the title on the page followed by two hard returns ¶, followed by author name, or pseudonym. Font should be Times New Roman 22 point.

My Life as Jane¶

¶

Jane Doe

Front Matter

Front matter includes the Dedication, Acknowledgements, Preface, Introduction, Prologue, etc. Titles should be centered followed by two hard returns ¶. A page break should be inserted at the end of each section. These elements are not usually numbered as part of the manuscript.

If you insist on numbering the pages of a prologue, the prologue should be a separate section. Go to the toolbar and select [Page Layout], expand the [Page Setup] area. In the [Section Start] window change it to New Page. You need to click on the [Insert] tab, click on [Insert Page Number], select [Bottom of The Page] then select Plain Number 2 which centers it at the bottom.

Once you have a page number at the bottom, you must modify it to Roman numerals by clicking on the [Insert] tab, click on [Page Number], click on [Format Page Numbers], in the box change the style to small case Roman numerals: i, ii, iii. Unselect the [Continue from Previous Section]. Then select [Start At] and enter 1.

You'll need to change the page numbers for your first chapter to begin with 1. You do this by making the first chapter a separate section. To do so click on [Page Layout], expand [Page Setup], click on the [Layout] tab, under Section Start change Continuous to New Page. Then go to [Insert] click on [Page Number] and choose the option for Bottom of Page, Plain Number 2. which places the number centered on the bottom of the page.

📄 Header

To insert a header, you need to start on the first page of Chapter One. If you made Chapter One a new section after numbering the prologue, you can proceed to the next step.

If you haven't, Chapter One needs to be made a new section so the header does not show up on the previous pages. To do this, click on [Page Layout], click on [Page Set-up], then click on the [Layout] tab. Change Section Start from Continuous to New Page. Then return to the toolbar and click on [Insert] then [Header]. You do not need to worry about a footer. The page number is the footer. On the Header menu, change the following fields:

Check: different first page so the header does not show up on the title page.

Check: Vertical alignment

Apply to: whole document

Font: Times New Roman 12

Paragraph Alignment: Center

Type your last name and Book Title.

Doe   The Places We Will Go

Make sure you don't have any hard returns ¶ in the header. It will give you odd line spacing.

▤ Special Offsets

If you have paragraphs that you want to format differently such as dream sequences, letters, poems, diary entries, news articles, etc. you can do so by offsetting it with a hard return ¶ before and a hard return ¶ after it.

To indent the entry, highlight the text in question. Go to [Page Layout], expand [Paragraph], go down to Indentations and change Left to 0.5 and Right to 0.5 and check the mirror indents box.

Do not change the font type, but you can use italics. This is discouraged. Readers have a tendency to skip over italicized elements unless they are riveting.

📄 Scene Breaks

To illustrate a scene break enter a hard return ¶, type five asterisks centered on the page with a space between each one, followed by a hard return. It should look like this with Reveal Codes turned on:

*. *. *. *. * ¶

If there are only two or three paragraphs between scene breaks, ask yourself why. It's possible you didn't craft your scene effectively. A scene should be five to ten pages. You can get away with three pages or fifteen. Short beats annoy rather than entertain. Some authors thrive on one paragraph or one sentence chapters. Most readers wish to slap them. It's lazy writing. A scene has a function. It has a beginning, middle, and an end. It examines a conflict, attempts to solve it, and offers a resolution. You can't pull that off in a paragraph.

📄 Special Characters

If you wish to insert special characters such as an em-dash or ellipsis, do so by clicking on [Insert]. [Symbol]. [Special Characters]. Do not type three periods or two dashes.

📄 Numbers

When writing numbers less than one-hundred, spell them out (i.e. twenty-five). For 100 or greater, use numerals. Unless you are using them in dialogue, in which case all numbers are spelled out: *"I sold one million books!"*

📄 Chapter Headings

Make sure you've inserted a page break after the last line of the previous chapter so that the chapter begins on a new page. Enter a hard return ¶, type the chapter title, center it, enter a hard return ¶. Do not start it halfway down the page.

📄 Back Matter

Additional pages such as indexes, reading lists, reading group questions, About the Author, notations, illustration guides, ads for others book in a series, etc. may be added to upload versions. Typically, agents and editors do not expect these additions from fiction writers. If used in the upload version, you will format them according to the entity's specifications. If formatting for PDF printing, the back matter should be a new section so the header doesn't show up. The pages should still be numbered.

📄 Proofreading Formatting

Turn on Reveal Codes by clicking on the icon ¶ on the toolbar. As you read through, this is your opportunity to remove extra spaces, tabs, returns, etc. At the end of each chapter, you should insert a page break which looks like this:

--Page Break--

At the end of each paragraph you should have a hard return, which looks like this: ¶.

Look for extraneous spaces which will look like this: ··." Each space is a dot ·.

Make sure you are viewing the document at its widest by clicking on [View] and selecting Page Width. It makes finding errors so much easier. Your eyes will thank you.

Formatting for E-Books

Open a new document. Save it as *Your Title for (Kindle)*.

Turn off automatic formatting. Click on the **[Word]** icon at the top left of the screen. Click on **[Word Options]**. Click on Proofing. Click on [Autocorrect Options]. Turn them all off and save, then return to the new document.

Open your manuscript file. Click [Control] [A], or Select All. Click Copy or [Control] [C]. Go to your new document. Place the cursor at the top of the page and select Paste Unformatted Text. Save it. Then go back and close your original file. What you now have is an unformatted stream of words. This is what you need to begin.

E-book files are not like the formatted manuscript you send to an agent or editor, nor do they resemble the formatted template you would upload to Create Space or another Print on Demand publishing platform.

E-book files must conform to whatever device they are read on, whether it is a tiny smart phone, an I-pad, or an E-reader. Therefore, you must eliminate all but paragraph breaks ¶ and, in some cases, page breaks at the end of chapters. The E-file does not incorporate headers, footers, page numbers, fancy fonts, indexes, or tables of content. Images can be imbedded by [Insert] [Image], but it is tricky. There are ways to code an index and a table of contents, but I'd leave that to the professionals.

It may seem like more work to start with a clean, stripped file, but it eliminates the bugaboos lurking in your manuscript that turn your E-book into hieroglyphs and cause weird page breaks.

Turn on Reveal Codes by clicking on the ¶ symbol in the toolbar. You can't ensure the format is correct without doing so. Viewing it at its widest by clicking on [View] and selecting Page Width makes identifying the dots and squiggles much easier. If you went through this editing process with your edited manuscript, you are half-way home.

The best font is Arial 12. You can use italics and bold. Some allow centering. Click Control A to select all the text. Change the font on the toolbar to Arial 12.

Kindle's conversion tool recognizes page breaks. Barnes & Noble's Pubit (Nook) does not. Smashwords has its own set of rules.

For Kindle, go ahead and insert a page break at the end of each chapter.

For Nook, use four hard returns ¶ at the end of each chapter.

... end of chapter one. ¶

¶

¶

¶

¶

Chapter Two

For both platforms, go to the top of the document. The chapter title or section title should be followed by two hard returns ¶.

Chapter One¶

¶

Go through the manuscript carefully. Make sure your chapters flow in one smooth stream with extra returns or page breaks only when required. Remove extra spaces, tabs, indents, etc. if they are present. Make sure you have it single spaced and left justified.

It is important to save your document in Word as **.doc** instead of **.docx**, though this may change as technology progresses. The document you create will then be converted to other formats by Pubit, the Kindle converter (which you must download, it's free), or Smashwords.

How you upload and convert the file varies with each entity. To follow their guidelines visit:

Kindle: https://kdp.amazon.com/self-publishing

Barnes &Noble Pubit:

https://simg1.imagesbn.com/pimages/pubit/support/pubit_epub_formatting_guide.pdf

Smashwords:
http://www.smashwords.com/books/download/52/1/latest/0/0/smashwords-style-guide.pdf

Formatting for PDF Print

Amazon's Create Space allows you to upload a formatted PDF version for print in Trade Paperback. Their instructions are more complex, but they offer templates to follow. This is not for absolute beginners. I would consider it intermediate level, if not expert level. If you do not have a healthy grasp of *Word for Windows*, take advantage of Create Space's conversion services. They charge for it, but it's worth it if you want to save yourself aggravation and disappointment. Create Space now has an online previewer, which allows you to virtually flip through the proof to make sure it is exactly as you would like. It also offers you multiple opportunities to proofread the file before you order the printed proof.

To check out Create Space PDF templates, visit:

https://www.createspace.com/en/community/docs

If you are familiar with PDF, HTML, or In Design, format away. Whatever you format in Word should translate into PDF in terms of fonts, headers, images, symbols, boxes, shading, italics, capitals, lists, columns, etc. I still recommend beginning with Create Space's templates then altering them as you see fit. This way you don't have to try to calculate page size, gutters, and correct margins. The templates already have a few chapters set up, the sections defined, and page setup done for you. Once you understand the basics of the templates, you can customize them in artistic ways. Download the templates and don't be afraid to play with them.

You can use whatever fonts you want, within reason. If you are using the fonts that came with Word, you are probably safe. If you downloaded a bunch of fancy fonts, symbols, and dingbats, you need to find out if you have permission to use them. They all came with licensing files you probably ignored. When you have converted your file to PDF, remember to check the fonts. Open the PDF version. Go to [File]. [Properties], click on the Fonts tab. You will be able to see if the font embedded successfully. If it didn't, you must go back and change the font in the original file. Delete this test document to avoid confusion later.

Images are a licensing and copyright issue. If you created the artwork or photo, you are free to use it. If you paid for the use of the image or downloaded a royalty free image and manipulated it, you are probably free to use it. Restrictions may have been placed on the usage of the image. If you decided you liked something you saw on the internet and saved it to your hard drive, you don't have permission to use it. If someone created artwork for you, you should get him to sign a release or give you written permission to use it, to legally protect yourself.

It is import to insert images using [Insert] [Picture] rather than copying and pasting them. Remember, when you adjust the size by dragging it, you change the dpi. If this sentence confuses you, you need assistance. Images should be at least 300 dpi. If you alter the size, do so through the [Picture] [Properties] section.

You could bribe, coerce, or sweet-talk a friend, relative, or teenager, who has the required skills to format the template for you. Teens are taught *Photoshop* and PDF in high school these days. There are individuals that advertise conversion services, but they aren't certified by any of the entities. It is a gamble to hire them. I would research the service provider thoroughly before considering it.

To use the Create Space's *Word* templates, create and edit your first draft and revise in *Word.* I don't recommend composing your first draft within the template. If you do, it will be filled with hidden formatting bugaboos that will bite you when you attempt to upload it. Copy text only into the Create Space *Word* template and change the fonts after. It requires a strong understanding of formatting in terms of adding chapters, front matter, back matter, indexes, table of contents, and changing font styles. If you know anything about the Styles section of *Word*, you can utilize that tool to full advantage.

The Create Space templates are *Word* documents. When you are happy with the results, save it and print it out. Read it through more than once. Make corrections. Read it through again. Then you can upload your file **.pdf, .doc, .docx,** or **.rtf.** Create space has a previewer that simulates what your book will look like so you can proofread it as many times as you like before committing to sending the files on for review.

Don't skip ordering a printed proof, and a second, perhaps a third. It doesn't matter how many times you have proofread the document electronically. The print version illuminates errors you've missed. When your printed proof is as clean as you can make it, then hit "submit."

FINAL THOUGHTS

I hope the revision passes discussed in this book help you polish your work to a high gleam. I know they have helped me immeasurably.

Revising may make you wish to quit and go spearfishing in Fiji. You may find me there ahead of you.

Writing is hard work. Revising your work is harder. It's worth it, or you wouldn't have read this book. Keep writing and polishing. Life is too short for bad fiction.

Diana Hurwitz

Index

[Automatic Formatting], 12
[Proofing], 13
[Require], 13
[Undo], 11
[Word Options], 12
Abstraction, 271
Action, 47
action and reaction, 32
Actions and Reactions, 21
adjectival clause, 179
Adjectives, 167
adverbs, 217
Alliteration, 271
Amplification, 272
Anadiplosis, 272
Analogy, 272
Anaphora, 272
Antithesis, 273
Apostrophes, 331
Assonance, 273
assumption of sameness, 65
Asyndeton, 273
Back Matter, 399
Backstory, 131
Balance, 273
basic sentence, 293
body language, 99
   anger, 108
   contempt, 109
   disgust, 109
   distance and touching, 104
   eye contact, 113
   facial expressions, 107
   fear, 109
   gestures, 111
   happiness, 110
   lying, 113
   reaction beats, 101
   sadness, 110
   surprise, 111

Brackets, 333
capitalization, 307
cause and effect, 29
character description, 63
Chiasmus, 273
Chronicity, 274
Cliché, 21
clichés, 233
collective noun, 162
Colloquialisms, 255
Colons, 335
Comma splices, 340
Commas, 337
Complexity, 22
compound sentence, 294
Conduplicato, 274
Conjunctions, 225
Connectives, 225
Consecutive, 274
Contractions, 343
Correlatives, 228
Create Space templates, 403
cultural shorthand, 149
Cumulative sentences, 298
Dashes, 344
Dead Zones, 22
Description, 47
Devices that Hook, 22
Dialogue
   Cadence, 77
   content, 86
   delivery, 77
   dialect, 78
   Education, 86
   enunciation, 79
   formatting, 69
   Inflection, 80
   pacing, 82
   pattern, 82
   Pitch, 84

tags, 75
tone, 85
   word choice, 86
Dreams, 136
Emotions, 47
Epanelepsis, 274
Epistrophe, 274
Epizeuxis, 275
false suspense, 147
flashback, 139
formatting, 391
Gerund phrases, 184
Goalposts, 23
Grammar, 14, 153
header, 396
High speed, 25
hook, 20
hooks, opening and closing, 21
Hyperbole, 275
Hyphens, 346
Hypophora, 275
Idioms, 233
In Media Res, 23
Infinitive phrases, 184
Interior monologue, 94
Interiority, 93
Interjections, 283
Isocolon, 275
Italics, 347
Jargon, 256
Kindle, 400
Line of sight, 36
Litotes, 276
Medium Speed, 25
Memories, 139
Metaphors, 276
micro-expressions, 107
Modifying Nouns, 157
Modifying phrases, 183
mood, 59
Narrative summary, 45
Narrative Summary, 24

narrator intrusion, 143
Negation, 218
Nook, 400
nouns, 155
omatopoeia, 287
omniscient, 63
opening and closing hooks, 21
Outcome, 24
Oxymorons, 276
Parallelism, 277
Parenthesis, 349
Participle phrases, 183
periods, 349
Personification, 277
persuasion plot hole, 119
persuasion techniques, 121
Phatics, 277
Plausibility, 35
Plot devices, 43
plot holes, 10
Plurals, 319
point of view, 51
   first person, 52
   first person subjective, 53
   objective third person, 54
   omniscient, 54, 63
Point of view
   Modified Objective Third Person, 53
Polyptoton, 279
Polysyndeton, 279
Preditors & Editors, 7
Prefabs, 279
prepositional phrase, 157
Prepositional phrases, 184
Prepositions, 189
Profanity, 261
pronouns, 155
Pronouns, 159
Proofreading, 305
Proper Nouns, 158
Punctuation marks, 331
Purple prose, 234

redundancy plot hole, 41

Redundant words, 265

relative clause, 179

repetitive words, 369

rhetorical devices, 271

rise, impact, and fall, 26

scene, 19

Scene Breaks, 398

Scenes, 17

search and kill, 10

Semi-Colons, 353

sentence beats, 292

sentence fragment, 295

sentence run on, 297

sentence structure, 291

Setting Errors, 24

Show versus tell, 45

Simile, 280

Slang, 257

Slashes, 357

Smashwords, 400

Speed, 25

speed bumps, 8, 10

Speed, high, 25

Speed, medium, 25

Speed, slow, 25

Speed, top, 26

Style, 14

subject verb agreement, 207

Suspense, 26

Symploce, 280

Synecdoche, 280

Telling, 47

Timing Errors, 27

tone, 57

Top speed, 26

Transitions, 229

Tricolon, 281

use this not that, 361

verb phrase, 213

Verb tense, 197

verbs, 191

    passive, 193

    weak, 194

Zeugma, 281

411

Diana Hurwitz

About the Author

Diana Hurwitz spent her childhood near Cincinnati daydreaming and writing poetry. She currently resides in Indianapolis with her husband, teen daughter, and two cats. She is a member of SCBWI, ALAN, Mystery Writers of America, and the Ladyscribes critique group.

For more information visit

www.dianahurwitz.com

OTHER WORKS BY THIS AUTHOR

Mythikas Island: Book One Diana

Mythikas Island: Book Two Persephone

Mythikas Island: Book Three Aphrodite

Mythikas Island: Book Four Athena

Story Building Blocks I:

The Four Layers of Conflict

If you missed the first book in the Story Building Block Series, it is available through Amazon.com & Barnesandnoble.com in print and e-book versions. It is available through your local bookstore on request.

Story Building Blocks II:

Creating Believable Conflict

If you enjoyed Story Building Blocks I, you will enjoy Story Building Blocks II in which we explore what makes your characters tick, and how to develop the conflicts that are central to your plot.

Story Building Blocks II:

The Companion

If you enjoyed Story Building Blocks II, you will enjoy Story Building Blocks II The Companion which features an in depth look at how each mannequin squares off with the other mannequins. To be released.